This is the Work:
Insights on Social Innovation and STEM Education

Zithri Ahmed Saleem
Trish Millines Dziko

Copyright © 2018 Technology Access Foundation.

All rights reserved. No part of this publication may be reproduced, distributed, or transmitted in any form or by any means, including photocopying, recording, or other electronic or mechanical methods, without the prior written permission of the publisher, except in the case of brief quotations embodied in critical reviews and certain other noncommercial uses permitted by copyright law.

ISBN: 978-1-71772782-4 (Paperback)
ISBN: 978-1-71772782-4 (ebook)

Front cover image by Tony Taj.

Printed by Amazon Press., in the United States of America.

First printing edition 2018.

> The Technology Access Foundation
> 605 SW 108th Street
> Seattle, WA 98146
> www.techaccess.org

Table of Contents

Acknowledgements i

Dedication iv

An Important Anti-Racist Preface v

Introduction 1

Part One: The History and Evolution of TAF 6

    TAF: The Early Years (1996 – 2004) 7

    TechStart: TAF Enters K-8 Space
    (2000 – 2005) 11

    TAF Academy: A Shift to Public Education
    (2005 – 2018) 12

    This is the Work: Storytelling and Public
    Scholarship 17

Part Two: A Crash Course in Relevant Theories ... 21

    Sociotechnical Perspectives 22

    Social Innovation 23

    Critical Perspectives on Technology 26

    Antiracism: Speaking Truth to Power 29

    Colonialism: Inclusion, Diversity, and
    Equity – WTF? 31

    Black Feminist Thought and Practice 34

**Part Three: Critical Conversations on Social
Innovation and STEM Education** 37

    Conversations with Trish Millines Dziko 38

Conversations with Dr. Nicole M. Joseph 62

Conversations with David D. Harris 83

Conversations with Sherrell Dorsey....................... 99

Part Four: Discussion on the Work Moving Forward 114

Knowledge Production and Sharing is "The Work"... 115

Conclusion 124

Appendix I: References 127

Appendix II: Reflection on "This is Work" by Zithri Ahmed Saleem 143

Acknowledgements

On behalf of the authors and contributors to this book, we are proud to stand on our ancestors' shoulders. We are forever thankful for the eternal love, guidance, and sacrifices of those who came before us, including countless scholars, educators, activists, and innovators across many generations. We consider ourselves in solidarity with all persons and spirits working toward antiracist, anti-oppression, decolonizing[1], and self-determination efforts – past, present, and future.

We extend thanks for the contributions of current and past staff, students, families, donors, corporate partners, and community supporters. We offer this book as a shared celebration of twenty-plus years of sustained labor and commitment to the growth and success of TAF students. As part of this celebration, we are grateful for the TAF Board of Directors for their patience and willingness to support the organic development of this project.

Much love and respect are due to each contributor to this book: Dr. Nicole Joseph, Sherrell Dorsey, and David Harris. TAF is indebted for their contribution of time, brilliance, and sustained

---

[1] The term "decolonizing" refers to the ongoing work of undoing widespread institutional dehumanization of nonwhite and Indigenous peoples that became globally pandemic under the era of European colonialism and continues today in various complex, ethnopolitical forms. (Fanon, 1963; Memmi, 1965; Smith, 1999; Tuck & Yang, 2012)

support for our students and families; both in their work at TAF and subsequently beyond. Proponents and advocates of social justice would be well-served to give their voices and work more attention and resources. It is indeed an honor to curate some of their insights and stories herein.

Domonique Meeks and Mayowa Aina – what else can be said? Their youthful energy and brilliance were invaluable throughout this project, whether building TAF's capacity to produce podcasts or helping to perform rigorous data collection and analyses for this book.

We extend gratitude to Tom Murphy, Sally McClean, and Josh Garcia. They were the Federal Way Public Schools (FWPS) leadership team that graciously welcomed TAF Academy into their school district in 2008. We also thank Carla Santorno, Aaron Wilkens, and our friends at Tacoma Public Schools (TPS) for their partnership and solidarity. All our district partners are instrumental in providing TAF access to leverage its experience and expertise in public school settings as opposed to less accessible out-of-school private programming.

We are thankful for the thought-leadership and collegiality of the University of Washington including Information School professors Negin Dahya, Ricardo Gomez, David Hendry, and Jason Yip; and professors Jean Dennison in the Department of Anthropology, and Carmen Rodriguez in the Department of Communications. Their support for Zithri Ahmed Saleem in his doctoral studies has been generous and appreciated.

Without question, this book is the result of a community effort. A tremendous thanks go to all the supporters of the "This is the Work" project on Kickstarter, including Kelly McNelis, Kris Kutchera, Jonathan & Mikka Hall, Ngoc Do, Elliott Coby, Stacey Childress, Ronald Howell, and Viren Kamdar. Their early gift of faith and patience were a much-needed boost to this effort.

We recognize generous and sustained contributions from numerous corporate and philanthropic partners including Social Venture Partners (SVP), Bill and Melinda Gates Foundation, the Paul G. Allen Foundation, the Ballmer Group, Microsoft, Google, Weyerhaeuser, Bruce and Jeannie Nordstrom, PACCAR, Boeing, Expedia, and Alaska Airlines.

Last but certainly not least, TAF would not be present today without the sustained support of Evelyne Rosner, Douglas Jackson, and many supporters and trusted advisors for Trish Millines Dziko. We are particularly grateful for the ongoing support and friendship of Ken Birdwell whose relationship with Trish predates her time at Microsoft. Before TAF ever opened its doors, Ken was a stalwart champion of TAF's vision and mission. A quiet sentinel in our communities for whom we are deeply appreciative.

Dedication

We dedicate this work to the memory of Paula Marcus, Luversa Sullivan and all Black women who have selflessly devoted their lives to empowering our communities through education and innovation. Above all, we dedicate this to our mothers. May eternal love, peace, and blessings be upon them all.

An Important Anti-Racist Preface

This book is no doubt evidence of TAF's unconventional approach to impacting its communities. For over 22 years, TAF has continuously defied mainstream logic and conventions while solving problems and developing tactics to deliver on its mission "to equip students of color for success in college and life through the power of interdisciplinary science, technology, engineering, and math (STEM) education and supportive relationships." Part of TAF's unconventionality is rooted in a deep familiarity with the adverse impacts that mainstream United States institutions have on nonwhite and Indigenous peoples (e.g., Black, Latinx, Native Nations, Asian Pacific Islander). Self-publishing this book, rather than a more conventional publication route, is consistent with TAF's legacy of working to get things done on its terms.

In 1996, TAF was a forerunner and common focal point of many national conversations at the intersection of race, education, and technology. At a time when most people saw technology as neutral, and the broad exclusion of nonwhite peoples from professional workplaces as seemingly natural, TAF boldly challenged the inequitable landscape and popular convention by centering "students of color" in its mission. It was unapologetic about its choice of language and programmatic focus. Many of TAF's early critics, skeptics, and allies alike, often commented that the explicit organizational focus on students-of-color would severely limit both private and public support for TAF programs. Perhaps worse, the same people cautioned, TAF's in-your-face mission could hamper the organization's real or perceived relevance to broader society. Nonetheless, TAF held steadfastly. Public awareness is much higher today. Many progressive educators, funders, policymakers, and business leaders widely acknowledge that "people of color" experience a broad range of inequitable outcomes across most social, economic, health, and educational metrics. *Anti-racist (or antiracist)* literature often illuminates how these outcomes are the result of mainstream methods, logic, and institutional practices that have privileged "whiteness" at the expense of nonwhite and Indigenous peoples for many generations (Hill Collins, 2010; Joseph, Haynes, & Cobb, 2016; Kendi, 2016; Noble, 2018; Patel, 2016; Smith, 1999). Institutional oppression of nonwhite peoples in the United States is frequently described as "white supremacy," a resurgent term that began to escape popular American vernacular after 1940's, but prior to, was an explicit aim of United States' global and domestic policy (Bonilla-Silva, 2001; Kendi, 2016; Marable, 1983; Mills, 1997). The current political climate in the United States has re-invigorated mainstream discussions about the extent to which white supremacy endures within our institutions, culture, and mindsets. A big question on the table for educators and those who value social justice is how can the current generation work to overcome the political, economic, and sociological forms of enduring white supremacy that undermine our schools and communities?

    It appears the so-called "race problem" and all its evolutionary complexities, as explained by Baldwin, Lorde, DuBois, and many others, is still the elephant in the room in 2018. Addressing it is a task that is much bigger than many of us are willing to recognize or admit, let alone do the work to solve or speak truth to it. For our part, TAF understands that continuous reassertion of the term white supremacy in antiracist literature helps to name and challenge the elephant in the room; namely, longstanding patterns of racist behaviors, practices, and logic that remain prevalent today, but often go unremarked in mainstream conversations of race, STEM, and social innovation. This book boldly reaffirms TAF's commitment to emancipatory and antiracist traditions by presenting voices and experiences from TAF community members in ways that challenge both conventional thinking and language patterns in these domains. This book makes a significant linguistic move and intentional pivot from using mealy-mouthed terms such as "diversity," "inclusion," "students of color," "minorities," and "underrepresented" which tend to hide the roles of power, history, and racialized hierarchies in our society. Instead, to support clarity and meaning-making, we move toward more appropriate and precise terms such as white, nonwhite, impoverished, antiracism, patriarchy, and white supremacy to describe our peoples, work, impacts, and contexts.

    This book – the first of many expected to be published by

TAF – aspires to be an accessible gateway to more in-depth, critical conversations and perspectives about STEM education, technology, and social innovation. The contents spring from TAF's knowledge and organizational experiences combating the patterns of white supremacy in STEM education, by both study and experience. For the sake of clarity, it is important to note that in 1996 when TAF was founded, mainstream digital divide literature still discussed technology and the Internet as social equalizers that might democratize knowledge and public education, ultimately providing widespread access to emerging innovation markets across race, gender, and class. The last twenty-plus years of mainstream digital culture and technology development, however, have given us significant reasons to temper any unbridled optimism for technology's potential to close societies' most profound social schisms. Racist and gendered stereotypes and biases have surfaced in search engines, artificial intelligence, and facial recognition algorithms, evincing the persistence of both white supremacy and patriarchy as normative functions, and outcomes, of mainstream technology development (Eubanks, 2018; Nakamura, 2002; Noble, 2018). The indictment speaks directly to the complicity – intentional or not – of technology companies and their supporting institutions, from the government to venture capital, and even the broader public in perpetuating and reproducing a nasty gamut of gendered and racialized social and structural inequities, both in digital and analog environments.

Our citizenship and daily participation in society make us all complicit in reproducing inequities to varying degrees that may be known or unknown to us. Some of us, however, exercise more discretionary power than others in our making daily choices and influencing institutional behavior to either contribute to or combat, inequitable momentums – this is a core idea behind the term, "privilege." Thus, considering our respective privileges, each of us – especially us technophiles and technology creators – should all pause from our frenetic, algorithm-driven lives and question, why has the broad socialization of technology into our schools, homes, cars, and intimate spaces coincided with record-setting profits for corporations and steadily expanding wealth-inequality? Why are health, educational, economic, and sociopolitical outcomes today overwhelmingly consistent with longstanding patterns of racialized and gendered oppression of nonwhite peoples, despite technological advancement? What roles do, or might, STEM education, technological development, and social innovation play in reproducing or reversing social and institutional inequities?

"The Work" referred to in this book's title starts with naming and recognizing the problem for what it is. Just as no rational person would ever think it possible to discuss alcoholism without understanding and referencing addiction; neither is it possible to discuss social and institutional inequities between "races" in the United States without being critically engaging in the logic, language, and mechanisms of white supremacy – it is a baseline matter. Now approaching twenty-five years of operation, TAF has sustained its bold focus of educating many students racialized as nonwhite, and white, alike, according to a vision for a more sustainable and equitable future made possible through STEM. This book doubles down on that focus. Equally important, TAF has developed its success by cultivating broad-based community partnerships across sectors, including many advocates that are unwavering in their support for TAF's work including the development of this book.

Introduction

By Zithri Saleem

"To equip students of color for success in college and life through the power of interdisciplinary science, technology, engineering, and math (STEM) education and supportive relationships." – TAF Mission Statement

Knowledge is embedded in the stories we tell – both to others and ourselves. The TAF community is a diverse network of scholars, practitioners, and community members with core values centered around empowering communities through STEM education and social innovation. This book is an act of organizational storytelling that seeks to share insights and perspectives developed from a series of conversations with influential members of the TAF community.

As a senior leader in the TAF community, it is essential to be both transparent and reflexive about our processes for how we approached the development of this book before proceeding into the more profound insights and discussion. My identity and relationship to TAF and other contributors to this effort is relevant to how we present the views and findings herein. In clarifying my positionality, my intention is not to introduce myself as neutral, or objective, by any means. I agree with advocates of decolonizing methods including Linda Tuhiwai Smith (1999) in believing that objectivity is not a meaningful goal that one should aspire to in work with, and research of, nonwhite, colonized, and Indigenous peoples. Instead, my intention and mindset in bringing this book forward are to honor the experiences, voices, and stories of its contributors in ways that are recognizable to their tellers. I aim to curate them in accessible ways that might offer current and future value, both to TAF and similarly situated communities. The audience we have in mind is anyone who is actively engaged in, or considering, the work of affecting social change through STEM education, technology, or social innovation. This book offers an exploratory treatment of questions such as, "What roles do identities play in how community members approach social innovation and STEM education?," "How do we think about antiracist, decolonizing, and anti-oppression approaches in these domains?," and "How do community members value various types of frameworks, structures, practices, experiences, and mindsets our work?"

Trish Millines Dziko and I continuously reflected on the best ways to create this work as a reflective exercise. It was important to us that this book builds upon TAF community voices and experiences, so we tapped deep into our networks, conducted over forty-three (43) hours of interviews, including collecting the views and experiences of current and former TAF students, teachers, caregivers, staff, donors, and the broader community. Interviews were transcribed, coded and re-coded for common themes. We also reviewed a selection of critical artifacts including old press articles, internal documents, photographs, and digital assets such as video, audio, and web materials. These materials were not coded but were instrumental to our overall analyses. I experimented with and borrowed from a mixture of narrative, case, and ethnographic research methods over a two (2) year period 2016-2018 to formally conceptualize and develop this reflective-study.

The more significant part of our analyses draws on my 20-years of lived experience as an educator and social entrepreneur in my community. I undertook the formal task of writing this book with the sole charge of collecting and developing the narratives herein with continuous support from Trish and other contributors in the form of periodic conversations and interviews. The ideas presented in this book echo their stories, reflections, and insights. *Narrative research* is relatively young, but a fast-growing qualitative approach suitable for intimately exploring individual stories (Connelly & Clandinin, 1990; John W. Creswell, 2007; Ollerenshaw & Creswell, 2002). Kourti (2016) examines the role(s) of personal narratives in organizational identity. Using interviews with corporate stakeholders, Kourti (2016) concludes that personal narrative approaches allow for multiple organizational identities to emerge and that knowledge of these identities can be useful in organizational decision-making and broader knowledge-production. Using narrative methods enable us to see that there is not one monolithic *TAF Story* but multitudes of *TAF stories*, of which, only a small but purposive fraction is included in this book. We do not claim that the selected stories are representative of all TAF stories, and we fully acknowledge that other worthwhile narratives and even organizational counternarratives exist.

A significant point of emphasis in this text is a direct sharing of community voices. These voices provide detail and richness around several themes that emerged in the analysis of our data including social innovation, asset-based community development, organizational development, critical pedagogy, leadership, design, learning communities, and hacking. In interviewing Trish each week, we would reserve a portion of our time to discuss the overall research design and process and reflect on any new insights or understandings we had resulting from our conversations or others. Part of the work was mapping and retelling Trish's and other contributors' narratives into a broader statement on community storytelling and values. Trish's name appears as a co-author of this book, firstly, in deference to her enduring commitment to the students and families of the TAF community, and secondly, for her sponsorship of this book effort against the grains of conventional wisdom. This authorial attribution is done intentionally in defiance of traditional logic and conventions around ownership of knowledge and its modes of production. To be clear, I believe that "knowledge" is a co-constructed phenomenon that exists beyond the confines of individualism that preoccupy popular imagination. While I have been privileged and instrumental in the academic production of the contents within this text, Trish has been a co-author of the worldly conditions that facilitated the development of this book.

Regarding the organization, I have divided this text into four parts not including this introduction; and is not necessarily meant to be read cover-to-cover. Readers should engage it in ways that make the most sense them as there are different types of readers and various reasons why someone might take up this text as a reading. "Part One: The History and Evolution of TAF" lay out core events, ideas, and details that are necessary for putting the remainder of this book in context. "Part Two: Key Concepts and Theories" offers an overview of relevant theories and perspectives that are helpful in considering TAF and its work. "Part Three: Critical Conversations on Social Innovation and STEM Education" shares the ideas and stories of four influential TAF community members: Trish Millines Dziko (Executive Director and Co-Founder), Dr. Nicole M. Joseph (Professor of Mathematics Education, Vanderbilt University), David D. Harris (Startup Advocate, City of Seattle), and Sherrell Dorsey, (CEO and Co-Founder of The Plug Daily and Black Tech Interactive). "Part Four: Discussion on the Work Moving Forward" brings together the stories of the contributors and additional members of the TAF community to suggest ideas and questions for current and future work in STEM education and social innovation.

Part One: The History and Evolution of TAF

This section provides a foundation for understanding TAF as an organization including key events, concepts, contexts, and vocabulary referenced throughout the remainder of this book. This section situates TAF and this book within its significance to mainstream discussions on STEM education and social innovation, and broader society. One of the most important things this introduction does is to make clear vital relationships between the authors and contributors of this book. It surfaces shared values and meaningful experiences we collectively bring into our different works as educators, technologists, researchers, hackers, data journalists, and ecosystem developers. The end goal of this introduction is to set the stage for a meaningful exploration of the insights and stories that are shared by authors and contributors in subsequent parts of this text.

TAF: The Early Years (1996 – 2004)

Just over twenty (20) years ago, TAF was founded as a small nonprofit in Seattle with a mission aimed at closing the *digital divide*. Around that time, there was relatively little mainstream attention to nonwhite communities' inequitable access to computing technologies and STEM-related economies. Most organizations with national reach such as Code.org, CODE2040, and Girls Who Code, were nonexistent and the same can be said for many university and college-based STEM outreach programs. At the academic level – research that investigated access to technology and related economies for different groups based on factors such as class, race, gender, and geographic location was also relatively nascent. Thus, when TAF stepped onto the scene in 1996, it did so as an early intervener in the national landscape of digital divide without many other organizations from which it could take explicit lessons. To keep it simple, TAF was a pioneer.

TAF launched in 1996 with the Technical Teens Internship Program (TTIP), an after-school program focused on providing digital literacy and programming skills to nonwhite students in central and south Seattle. The early days of TAF were all about getting nonwhite students into internships at top companies in Seattle's thriving technology sector. For the sake of context, it is highly valuable to establish that in 1996, Seattle was not quite the global technology hub that it is today. Central and South Seattle areas were in the early stages of their gentrification.

Back then, the Central District (i.e., "CD") had a variety of Black-owned businesses and a predominantly Black and nonwhite demographic core. Almost none of which could anticipate just how fast the local technology sector was about to remake their neighborhoods and worlds. The "Shelf Life Project," a podcast series released in May 2018, offers a thoughtful post-mortem reflection about the rapid gentrification that took place throughout Seattle's Central District. Shelf Life podcasts are valuable to hear firsthand accounts of the rapid shift in Seattle's urban, nonwhite community life. Each podcast underscores just how much both nonwhite and white residents in the "CD" were caught off guard and subsequently displaced by rapid changes happening about them. It turns out, in hindsight, that while the entire city was captivated at the now-departed Seattle Supersonics face-off against Michael Jordan in the 1996 NBA finals, technology companies including Microsoft, Amazon, Nintendo, and Starbucks were growing in ways that disproportionately left many of Seattle's nonwhite peoples on the outside of looking in. These events contain no judgment; this is just facts. Trish Millines Dziko and her partner Jill Hull Dziko made early diagnosis of the problem, and TAF was their solution. Once the doors opened, TAF hired Sherry Williams who worked as Trish's Executive Assistant and quickly became her right-hand woman. Notably, Sherry remains as Trish's confidant until present-day and serves as TAF's Deputy Director.

In the early days of TAF, high school students would take

afterschool classes two-days a week for three (3) hours a day at either of the TAF locations. The original headquarters was a leased historic brick building in south Seattle's Columbia City neighborhood surrounded by many businesses and homes owned by working-class Black and nonwhite residents. In 1998, the TAF program, TTIP, grew to a second leased-space across town on 23rd and Judkins in the Central District. The "Judkins" space was acquired to accommodate larger enrollments and provide easier access to students coming from nearby Garfield and Franklin high schools – the two largest high schools in south-central Seattle. The internship program cohort sizes were nonetheless small, ranging from just ten (10) to as many as forty (40) students. The program served roughly seventy (70) students per year, and students who completed each year of training received an internship and a $1,000 scholarship toward college for each year they were in the program ($4,000 max). For comparison, in 1997, the in-state annual tuition at the University of Washington, the state's most expensive and elite public university, was $3,366. In 2018, the year of this publication, the same tuition is $10,753. In present-day dollars, the max TAF scholarship would be worth just under $13,000 – over one-year of tuition and fees. These tuition numbers provide an idea of how TAF was offering a significant financial incentive for participating students and families beyond skills and technical training. The scholarship incentive substantially reduced a significant barrier for many TAF students to access and afford a college education.

Nevertheless, the primary value TAF offered to students and families was not scholarships, but technical knowledge. The knowledge came with the confidence and experience of students seeing themselves as belonging in the broader technology ecosystem. This feat of "belonging" was achieved through participation in weekly classes and high-tech internships. Each TAF student gained access to technical content and industry skills as they learned to write code, repair hardware, administer networks, develop websites, and manage their time and coursework. TAF co-founder, Trish Millines Dziko, and volunteers initially taught TTIP classes, but by the second year of the program, it was clear that TAF needed a paid instructional team for scale and stability. That year, Trish hired an instructional team that included Larry Powelson, a fellow Microsoft retiree, Jason Boyd, a University of Washington student studying art and design, and Ian Hageman, a community educator-activist with a penchant for binary code, bicycles, and hardware. It is worthwhile to acknowledge that none of the original instructional or administrative staff had formal backgrounds in education or instruction, but they all shared deep passions for technology and a belief in the potential they could have on TAF students' lives. They were education-hackers, a theme revisited later in this text. Out of the gate, however, the TAF internship program delivered tremendous value to students and families. Employers raved about TTIP students' technical acumen and workplace readiness, and both local and national media were eager to cover the success of

Trish, the "Microsoft Millionaire" who was working to change the face of tech in the region. Media coverage contributed significantly to TAF's growth and recognition in through the nineties.

TechStart: TAF Enters K-8 Space (2000 – 2005)

In 2000, shortly after the Y2K global hysteria, TAF realized that students were excelling in internships, but many still struggled to become college-ready and college-eligible based on their academic coursework in school. The solution was to launch TAF's first kindergarten through the eighth-grade program, TechStart, to prepare students for both TTIP and college-preparatory coursework better. This is the juncture where I formally enter the story – as authorial curator for the remainder of this book and the inaugural TechStart Program Manager. With a few years of experience as a Math Tutor for college students with learning differences to my credit, I began my work with TechStart students focused on teaching essential math, critical thinking, and academic skills through technology. I stressed learning to become power-users in Microsoft Windows and Office, and how to build elementary mathematical and statistical models for predator-prey systems and basic differential equations. I had refined my math philosophy and pedagogy through continuous field-study and conversations with my mentors; Seattle math education icon, Norm Van Alston, and Dr. Nicole Joseph, a contributor to this book former math coach for Seattle Public Schools (SPS). Norm and Nicole championed a philosophy called advanced concepts early (ACE). Their guidance gave me confidence and know-how to push students beyond what they, their parents, or hardly anyone else imagined was possible, and yet, engage and support each of my students in nearly every step. By the end of the fifth-year of my work with TechStart, I had led the program from a fledgling pilot to a highly-regarded program among many Seattle parents and teachers. The program now had additional instructors and was serving over two-hundred (200) students per year at eight (8) sites throughout the greater Seattle area. Beyond mere technology, TechStart students were mastering competencies in core academic content areas and demonstrating their knowledge through complex projects and authentic exhibitions. In many ways, TechStart laid the foundation for TAF to begin to think differently about our expectations and approach for what we could accomplish with students in addition to internships and technical training. It is accurate to say, TechStart provided TAF the foundation for its future instructional philosophy around project-based STEM (i.e., STEM pedagogy).

TAF Academy: A Shift to Public Education (2005 – 2018)

By 2005, the impact of TAF programs was quickly catching the attention of local teachers, educators, community advocates, and funders. After several conversations around how to scale TAF's model and success, TAF eventually secured a commitment from the Bill and Melinda Gates Foundation's Small Schools Initiative. Small Schools were a school model centered on values such as personalization, site-based autonomy, and principals as instructional leaders rather than merely administrators. The Gates Foundation and the Paul Allen Foundation became TAF's lead investors in the effort to transition the organization from running after-school programs into operating a network of small schools. The plan was to launch the first "TAF Academy", a 6th-12th grade STEM school, in Fall of 2008. I was promoted to TAF Director of Education to lead the effort, where I served from 2005 until relinquishing the position in 2013.

The Center for Reinventing Public Education publication, Legal Issues and Small High Schools: Strategies to Support Innovation in Washington State (Warner-King & Price, 2004) heavily influenced the development of the TAF Academy model. This publication was significant on multiple levels. It is not a trivial detail that in 2008 when we launched TAF Academy, Washington State was among a handful of states whose laws did not sanction charter schools – though the state law currently sanctions them at the time of this publication. To grossly oversimplify, charter schools leverage public funds to operate schools independently managed from traditional public school districts. Charter schools remain a highly-contested issue in public education discourses. "Pro-charter" groups including many education reform advocates and charter management organizations (e.g., Rocketship Education, KIPP, Teach for America, Stand for Children) assert that charter schools are a necessary structure for much-needed innovation in public education. These groups often point to gaps in testing data and graduation rates between white and nonwhite students as evidence that public school districts have largely failed to serve all students equitably. Pro-charter groups contend that autonomy from traditional districts is required to take non-traditional approaches to education; whether deviating from traditional norms in school staffing, curriculum-and-content, teaching-learning-and-assessment, or leadership. On the other side of the charter debate, many community-based teaching organizations such as Rethinking Schools and Voices Against Privatization of Public Education see charters as an assault on public schools and teachers' unions. "Anti-charter" groups warn that a privatized, corporate-controlled public education system is dangerous to the idea of democracy. These groups often point to data, such as that provided in an American Civil Liberties Union (ACLU) report entitled, "How Some California Charter Schools Illegally Restrict Enrollment," which found that some charters in California had discriminatory admission practices (Leung, Alejandre, & Jongco, 2016). Anti-charter groups also see charter schools as detrimental to keeping teacher-driven educational practices free from the influence of corporate agendas which push de-unionization of labor.

Meanwhile, we developed TAF Academy as a *public-*

private partnership model. This new model leveraged existing laws to create autonomy and personalization for students and teachers but left taxpayer money in the hands of public districts. The TAF Academy model partnered with school districts to augment the basic funding that each school received from the state with additional private dollars. By the time we opened the doors of TAF Academy in 2008, we had 130 students registered to make the leap of faith with us, and we were at capacity in middle school with waiting lists. TAF Academy would grow to serve over 300 students annually by its third year.

    TAF Academy operated as a small, *public-private partnership school* as part of Federal Way Public Schools (FWPS) from 2008 until 2017. Seldom seen in public education, our "TAF Education" team was a young, energetic, and change-minded assemblage of mostly nonwhite engineers, lawyers, educators, human service workers, and technologists. We all worked together to design, develop, and breathe life into TAF Academy by supporting a staff of teachers and administrators to implement the TAF Academy project-based instructional model, working inside and outside of the classrooms with teachers, students, administrators, and families. In its short nine (9) year lifespan, TAF Academy graduated over 90% of its seniors with over 90% percent of them going on to attend college. The school won numerous regional and national awards for excellence and innovation, including the 2011 Innovation Award for Middle School Mathematics from the Intel Corporation for raising test scores 43% in one year; and, a 2011 Ashoka Changemakers, Partnering for Excellence award. These awards and several others helped place TAF Academy firmly on the radar of regional and national educators as a viable model or realizing equity-of-outcomes between nonwhite and white students. The TAF Academy operational and funding model did not scale into a network of schools as planned and this meant no additional TAF Academies. In 2017, TAF Academy was merged with another school Saghalie Middle School, to create TAF@Saghalie, getting TAF Academy students out of portables and into a full school building. This merger, effectively and controversially for many involved, pivoted TAF Academy from its small school roots, as TAF@Saghalie currently serves nearly 700 students.

Perhaps the biggest takeaway from this brief treatment of TAF's history is that the organization has experienced tremendous growth and development since its 1996 inception; from operating afterschool programs to co-managing the TAF@Saghalie public school. Today, TAF also partners with several school districts through its "STEMbyTAF" model which provides professional development and site support for teachers based on TAF Academy strategies. Also, TAF operates two teacher training and professional development programs, the STEMbyTAF Teacher Institute and the Martinez Fellowship, which leverage TAF knowledge and experience to prepare culturally and STEM competent, white and nonwhite, teachers to work in schools and districts throughout Washington State.

This is the Work: Storytelling and Public Scholarship

I first began thinking about developing a "TAF book" during my 16-year tenure alongside Trish Millines Dziko. For many years, I implored her to write a book that captured her story and our work at TAF. My thought was that writing a book about TAF's history and approach would be meaningful for like-minded educators. There were unique ways that our team was preparing nonwhite students to thrive in Seattle's technology-driven ecosystem, and at the time, TAF was regularly receiving national awards for our programs. As Director of Education, I had assembled an all-star cast of mostly nonwhite talent on our Education Team, a rarity in Seattle; as I understood that nonwhite students benefit from having teachers and role models with whom they share aspects of identity such as heritage, culture, language, and class (Banks & Banks, 2004; Emdin, 2016; Garibay, 2013; Watkins, 2005). My team included several people who would go on to become highly-respected STEM leaders at a national level. Our team's primary function was to support the school we had recently launched, TAF Academy, Washington State's first non-charter STEM school focused on nonwhite student achievement via a private-public partnership. Writing a book to make our work and approaches more visible seemed to make sense. And while our work was pioneering, it was also done on the shoulders of those that came before us. I wanted to pay it forward. Nonetheless, Trish's response to publishing a book was always lukewarm. In her mind, there was just too much work and not enough time or resources to warrant such an endeavor. Quietly, I considered it an opportunity lost – so I kept focused on the moment at hand, but never gave up on the idea. Just around the TAF 20th anniversary in 2016, Trish began to see the value. And so here we are.

In my experience, I have always looked at Trish through the lens great Black emancipatory leaders. I grew up in a Pan-Africanist community where we studied the philosophies and works of names like Hurston, Bethune, Davis, DuBois, Lorde, Shabazz, Nkrumah, Walker, Touré, Garvey, and Hughes. Before I was in sixth grade, I recall having to memorize selections of their works verbatim, perform public recitals, and participate in community debates around their intellectual contributions – from Garvey's views on Black nationalism to DuBoisian perspectives on race and capitalism. In my days at TAF, I imagined that people might one day consider the name "Trish Millines Dziko" within the pantheon of pivotal Black educators and activists. In one of our many conversations for this book, Sherrell Dorsey, TAF alumni and CEO of Black Tech Interactive and The Plug Daily, noted that Trish and TAF were "getting up shots" in 1996 when most folks had not even diagnosed the problem. Back then, diversity, inclusion, and equity had not yet become diluted corporate buzzwords as they are today. Instead, there was growing attention and debate around the "digital divide," a term popularized in the early 1990s to describe class-based disparities in computing and

Internet access, such as those that exist between white and nonwhite peoples, women and men[2], or rural and urban communities. In 1996, few people and community-based organizations were aggressively attacking the digital divide with the vigor and foresight of Trish and TAF. And even fewer of those that started around 1996 are still in operation today. It is no small feat that TAF is still here.

TAF's significance to the space of STEM education is not merely the numerous students that it has put on STEM college and career pathways, but equally important is the role that TAF has played in being a springboard and incubator for young, brilliant nonwhite educators and social entrepreneurs. Krige and Silber (2016) describe social entrepreneurs as "unreasonable" people who question the status quo and mobilize people and resources to improve social conditions. Social entrepreneurs are disruptive. The list of notable nonwhite educators and social entrepreneurs for whom TAF was a part of their genesis includes David D. Harris, Dr. Nicole Joseph, Dr. Robyn Viloria Wiens, Kia Franklin, Esq., Chris Alejano, and me. Each of us brought something special and unique to the TAF mission based on our identities, talents, personal commitments, and visions for our community and social change. More than anything else, the ideas

---

[2] TAF does not support a binary perspective of gender. The terms "women and men" is used to accurately reflect how popular digital divide discussions approached gender.

and labor that many other colleagues and we contributed to TAF programs are what has enabled TAF's success.

Furthermore, all of us have leveraged our TAF experiences and networks to exponentiate TAF's mission beyond the formal organization through our subsequent works in city government, industry, higher education, and public service. In this way, Trish and TAF have contributed to a multiplier effect regarding their impact on our communities far beyond direct services. Personally, in transitioning to becoming an academic researcher and writer, I considered it an honor to be an integral part of the extended TAF community and take up the challenging work of producing this book as one of my first acts of public scholarship.

Part Two: A Crash Course in Relevant Theories

This section offers essential context for considering TAF within relevant spheres of theoretical and public discussion. The writing developed during my first years of doctoral studies (2016 – 2018). Due to both time constraints and a nod to Hip-Hop culture that values having both raw (i.e., freestyle) and refined (i.e., studio) presentations of one's work in circulation, I have not overly revised or edited the contents as this book. It is intended as a reflective public-exhibition – meaning it is not designed to be a final product but an opportunity to solicit feedback and provoke meaningful community conversations. There is a notable roughness in some of the ways that I introduce and discuss various theoretical perspectives, and I have no doubt left plenty of gaps. We intend this section as a crash course of sorts, not a full exposition. Readers are encouraged to consult cited works for more thorough treatments of theories presented here. I am confident, nonetheless, that most readers will find this section accessible and informative, as many of the arguments and ideas presented are highly relevant not only to TAF, but for thinking broadly about the intersections of technology, social innovation, race, gender, and power within society. Please note the ideas introduced in this section are continuously revisited throughout the remainder of the text.

Sociotechnical Perspectives

This book, as did the Technology Access Foundation (TAF), begins with a specific concern: access to technology for nonwhite students. Part of this concern is rooted in the authors' and contributors' intimate familiarity with longstanding disparities between many nonwhite communities in the United States and their white counterparts. These disparities span many socioeconomic dimensions; from high-quality public education, economic opportunity, and healthcare, to fair and affordable housing, and civil protection under the law. Increasingly, it is helpful to look at these disparities as sociotechnical matters, meaning they exist at the intersection of human behavior and complex technical systems (e.g., networks, governments, industry, organizations). Sovacool and Hess (2017, p. 704) note that sociotechnical theories and concepts help explain "the adoption, use, acceptance, diffusion, or rejection of new technology." Meanwhile, innovation-oriented discourses tend to focus on how technologies are conceived, developed, and made available to the public (Almirall, Lee, & Majchrzak, 2014; Anna Stahlbrost, 2011; Stokes, 2011). It is important to understand that meaningful access to technology for communities of color – as innovators, owners, and producers, not merely users and consumers – is an critical sociotechnical matter inextricably linked to our communities' outcomes for wellness, economic stability, and self-determination.

Throughout twenty-plus years of operation in the Greater

Seattle area, TAF has seen firsthand how lack of meaningful access to technological tools and economies can lead to undesirable outcomes such as gentrification, food-and-housing insecurity, and displacement of nonwhite people and entire communities. Present-day disparities in access to technological tools and economies are both resultant from, and reproductive of, patterns of colonialism – a form of systemic oppression that continuously racializes people and communities to exploit their land, labor, and resources (see Loomba, 2015; Wolfe, 2006). Modern technology is also a value-laden phenomenon – meaning it tends to inhere the values (e.g., social, political, cultural) of its creators and those who exercise power over its infrastructure and diffusion (Duarte, 2017; Feenberg, 1991). Thus, it should not be a tremendous leap of logic for anyone to understand why the people and communities most adversely affected by sociotechnical, economic, and political disparities in the United States are disproportionately nonwhite and Indigenous. Against this adverse institutional landscape, *desirable* social innovation for nonwhite peoples can conceptualized as socio-technical processes that move society away from colonial legacies toward more equitable and balanced power relationships in society.

Social Innovation

Up until this point, I have used the term social innovation without providing a working definition, and that is with some intention.

For that, I look to my dear friend and mentor, Dr. Jeffery Robinson, Professor at Rutgers Business School and Academic Director of the Center for Urban Entrepreneurship and Economic Development (CUEED). Dr. Robinson offered an excellent explanation of social innovation during a recent interview I conducted with him for the "This is the Work" podcast series pilot. I had caught up with him while he was on the best (i.e., West) coast for an entrepreneurship summit at San Jose State University where he had taken the CUEED Pipeline to Inclusive Innovation (CUEED PII) on the road. We flew down to record the podcast on-site and talk with a national cast of professors, venture capitalists, business students, policymakers, and entrepreneurs. Defining social and inclusive innovation was a theme of the CUEED summit.

  According to Dr. Robinson, social innovation is when you apply a business or organizational model to a new idea, product, or service to create social change or social impact. For example, let's say you have a idea for how to purify polluted municipal water for urban populations in cities with failing infrastructure. You spend time developing your idea, prototyping it, and eventually arrive at something that works – that is an invention. If you put the product online and begin to sell it – this activity makes you an entrepreneur because you recognized an opportunity and organized resources (and perhaps people) to take advantage of it. According to Dr. Robinson, it is not until you figure out a sustainable go-to-market strategy to make that invention broadly accessible to the public that you begin to arrive at innovation. In other words, innovation requires distribution. Now, suppose your top buyers are people who live in cities that already have relatively good municipal infrastructure and clean water. That is innovation, but the social impact is minimal, perhaps unbalancing, and certainly not what you intended. It is only when your solution impacts a significant social (or environmental) problem for an affected population that we can begin to consider it social innovation.

Indeed, the subject of social innovation is a critical matter for nonwhite peoples. It carries with it the promise of combating mainstream conversations and practices that reproduce existing oppressions and inequalities. We live in a day when students and communities in the United States spend a significant amount of time plugged into online networks. These networks connect them to information and people all over the globe, and there are endless possibilities for how we could leverage our global connectedness and collective knowledge toward widespread wellness and economic stability. Innovation hubs such as Seattle, Silicon Valley, and Austin have become iconic for innovation, sweeping the country up in a vibrant *technicism* that espouses modern technology can, and eventually will, solve many of society's most enduring problems. Yet, as anyone who has spent significant time on popular platforms such as Facebook, Google, Twitter, or YouTube can tell you, not only has the increased use of mobile computing and online networks not solved any enduring social problems, but rather, the current state of popular technologies is presenting new challenges that often go underappreciated and unspoken in mainstream media and public discussions of technology innovation.

Critical Perspectives on Technology

Critical Theory, Black Feminist Theory, and decolonizing methods provide necessary insights for understanding the relationship between modern technology and the existing systems of power and oppression that continuously structure and restructure our communities. Critical Theory is a philosophical perspective that focuses on the reflective assessment of the ideologies and power relationships at work within a social context or phenomena. Critical theory examines social actors, events, and contexts from the standpoint of asking how is power acquired, distributed, and performed along factors such as race, class, gender, and ability. Feminist Theory is a form of critical theory that is, as the renowned writer, Feminist theorist, and cultural critic bell hooks (2000) wrote, "about women gaining equal rights."

Similarly, decolonizing methods are rooted in the continuous work to undo colonialism as an ongoing global project that seeks to exploit the land, labor, and resources of Native, Indigenous and colonized peoples (Al-Hardan, 2014; Fanon, 1963; Memmi, 1965; Patel, 2016; Smith, 1999). Scholars have leveraged critical theories, Black Feminist Theories, and decolonizing methods to show the evolution and exacerbation of malignant systems of power such as patriarchy, white supremacy, and ableism through popular technologies (Eubanks, 2011, 2018; Feenberg, 1991; Noble, 2018; Vaidhyanathan, 2011). From gender racism in search engines (Noble, 2018), to the use of private data and facial recognition algorithms for overreaching surveillance and discriminatory policing (Eubanks, 2011), popular technology and digital media are relevant sites that reproduce and inhere both malignant social values and institutional oppression. These far-reaching systems and their underlying values and logic must be recognized and challenged before we can ever begin to see significant movement in the widespread inequitable outcomes undermining this modern sociotechnical "golden" era.

Critical perspectives on technology are also valuable because they offer counter-narratives to mainstream industry and public discourses that zealously push technology as a panacea for all our social problems and advancement. Critical perspectives push back against unbridled technicism and offer scholarly critiques that illuminate how popular technology platforms and the companies behind them are not meaningfully focused on advancing social wellness; but rather intent on extracting profits from the human tendency towards sociality. From a critical lens, mainstream technology development momentums are not necessarily innovative, but merely reproductive of existing systems of oppression. Thus, it is vital for nonwhite and Indigenous peoples to understand, confront, and conscript technology discourses and development toward their own goals and interests. Being in the driver's seat of technological advancement is a big chunk of the actual work!

We must appreciate the fact that that human and social information networks predate modern information communication technology (i.e., ICT). Information networks describe the various structures, processes, and protocols that people and societies have used to create, exchange, and store information, including telegrams, faxes, train systems, trade routes, schools, or families. Today, the Internet is the main information network which connects over 3 billion inhabitants of the earth – or, roughly half of the world's total population. Critical perspectives on technology point out the perils of having human information networks that are owned, controlled and nearly monopolized by elite corporate and state actors (Berry, 2014; Feenberg, 1991, 2002; Jordan, 2015; Nakamura & Chow-White, 2012). In the United States, many scholars are growing increasingly concerned with the current sociotechnical paradigm whereby technology companies covet our every thought, interaction, and movement as sources of potential data that might be continuously collected and harvested for corporate commerce and government surveillance (see Berry, 2014; Eubanks, 2011, 2018; Feenberg, 2002; Sandoval & Fuchs, 2010). For many critical observers, it seems that Western Liberalist ideals such as safety, privacy, equality, and freedom that were extolled by iconic philosophers such as Locke, Mill, and Rawls during the period of European Enlightenment have all but vanished. Once the ideals that inspired the United States founders, they are now only relevant to the extent that they might be commodified, sold, or used to support corporate or state interests online.

Meanwhile, well-meaning people often lead mainstream corporate tech rhetoric around diversity, equity or inclusion, but miss their mark because they lack critical insight into pertinent matters of race, power, gender, and class that shape the complex ways technology shows up in our daily lives. Simply stated, corporate "D&I" efforts are invariably underinformed, to say the least. And while in-depth discussion about what informs the corporate approach is beyond the scope of this book, the idea that technology is neither neutral, nor are its creators, nor impacts on nonwhite and Indigenous communities is essential to understanding the dominant sociotechnical landscape that is the context for TAF and similarly situated organizations' work.

Antiracism: Speaking Truth to Power

The current national climate makes it evident, more so than ever, that perceived advances and movements toward equality for nonwhite peoples, sociotechnical or otherwise, can expect to be met with immediate and violent backlash from those still holding on to segregationist ideologies and practices; including individuals, groups, and institutions. White supremacy is, after all, as American as baseball and apple pie. Many Americans, because of their stake in the current system of inequality, repeatedly attempt to intellectually justify the inequitable actions and outcomes of United States institutions as being merely happenstance, natural, or the "unfortunate" order of things (see Lipsitz, 1998). Segregationist ideologies assert that there are inherent differences in peoples' ability and values based on factors such as race and gender which hold explanatory power for the inequalities we see in society (Kendi, 2016). Negative stereotypes and myths about nonwhite people, their cultures, religious beliefs, and ways of living are an active part of the mainstream public imaginary that get continuously reinforced by digital and corporate media (Nakamura & Chow-White, 2012). The current President of the United States (POTUS) instantiates and encourages this same type of negativity when they Tweet or are heard on mainstream media making patriarchal white supremacist remarks about "low IQ people," "shithole countries," and "nasty" women. The vile and unpresidential behavior reinforces the point that nonwhite people, and even more so nonwhite women and Femme persons, face overwhelming circumstance in navigating the complex sociotechnical landscape that is the context in which our communities and peoples are situated. This same behavior directs and sanctions institutional and other forms of violence (e.g., physical, psychological, emotional) against nonwhite peoples, even from the highest levels. POTUS is not alone.

Increasingly, organizations like TAF along with our allies and accomplices, must shift our work and focus; from merely providing access to traditional college and career pathways that feed into the corporate sociotechnical systems and schemes, toward realizing new models and relationships for social innovation that are fundamentally antiracist and anti-oppressive. Eubanks (2011) prescribes "technology for people" as an inclusive and anti-oppression approach to technology innovation. The TAF vision for social innovation builds on the spirit of Eubanks' approach. It calls for the creation of alternative systems, ways of being, doing, and knowing that leverage the development and conscription of new and existing technology toward the urgent project of decolonizing and rebuilding our communities. Admittedly, this is no small task; however, this is also "the work."

Colonialism: Inclusion, Diversity, and Equity – WTF?

Although TAF uses the term "of color" in its mission, and other contributors to this book use the terms "Black and Brown," I use the term "nonwhite" interchangeably. This substitution is done to be more consistent with contemporary voices from Critical Race Theory, Black Feminist Theory, and decolonizing methods. In using any of these terms, the goal is never to assert any sort of homogeneity over the various peoples racialized as nonwhite. The substitution is only to recognize that in very different ways, peoples including Black, Latinx, Native Nations, Filipinos, and Indigenous peoples in the United States share a common experience of being exploited for their lands, resources, and labor to support U.S. economic and technological growth. A fact true from the time of the country's inception to the present day. Critical scholarship often discusses these exploitative acts and their impacts under the broad heading of *colonialism* (Bonilla-Silva, 2017; Loomba, 2015, 2015; Memmi, 1965; Stefancic, 1997; Wolfe, 2006). Whereas mainstream discourses often omit or punctuate the United States history chapter on colonialism in the last century, critical scholarship argues that U.S. colonial practices have evolved into present-day disparities between how many nonwhite people experience life and society compared to their white counterparts. These experiences include mass-incarceration of Black, Latinx, and Indigenous peoples in the U.S. prison-industrial complex (Alexander, 2010), inequitable access to high-quality public school education (Anderson, 2014; Shedd, 2015; Woodson, 2000), ongoing disruption of nonwhite families through political and physical violence (see Dunaway, 2003), and of course, exclusion of many nonwhite communities from meaningful participation in technology-driven economies.

There is a nuance to be explored here. Exclusionary practices are symptomatic and structural extensions of colonial systems and racist behaviors that stretch back centuries, which at their core, privilege white people and white communities at the expense of "others" racialized as "nonwhite." In *Racial Contract*, Charles Mills (1997) describes how the 18th century intellectual and philosophical movement in Europe that inspired United

States' founders did not consider nonwhite peoples as eligible participants in the social contract(s) that were being discussed by prominent thought-leaders including Rousseau, Locke, and Kant. This so-called period of "Enlightenment" extolled Liberalist ideas of individual rights, freedom, and equality but neglected to extend them to the majority of world's population who were deemed to be part of the *terra nullius* that was to be conquered and exploited for the prosperity of those of European descent (Memmi, 1965; Mills, 1997; Wolfe, 2006). Europeans constructed "Whiteness" as a race not merely as a biological classification for scientific or demographic purposes, but primarily as a political classification that facilitated and rationalized the dehumanization and colonization of populations deemed as "nonwhite" (Painter, 2010; Sakai, 2014; Wolfe, 2006). Accordingly, it was possible and largely unquestioned in the imagination of European-decent authors of the United States Declaration of Independence, that they could proclaim "all men are created equal" in stern argument of their "unalienable Rights" to "Life, Liberty and the pursuit of Happiness," while at the same time administering the enslavement of Africans and the genocide of Native and Indigenous nations. And not to mention, the gendered subjugation of their "white" mothers and sisters. Fast forward to today, and you find complex sociotechnical issues of exploitation that disproportionately affect nonwhite peoples; from issues of unpaid digital labor on social media (see Scholz, 2013), to the digital commodification of Black women's trauma online (see Maragh, 2016). My intention in conjuring these ugly histories and events is not to resuscitate trauma or trigger guilt, but rather to be explicit about the exclusionary logics and practices that typically evade discourses under the banners of "diversity," "inclusion," and "equity." Colonialism and its various manifestations are worth naming and understanding in clear terms rather than euphemistic rhetoric. We must ask, whose interests do the euphemisms serve and protect, and whose interest do they harm and hinder? The bottom line is we all need to move past them toward more powerful language and logic, fast.

Black Feminist Thought and Practice

It is impossible to have a meaningful conversation about race in the United States without an equally measured treatment of the experience of women – Black women. For example, the exclusion of women from full participation in the society is evident in early U.S. political documents, events, and discourses which largely focus on the rights of "men" and consider women as collateral property (Pateman, 1988). Meanwhile, hooks (1981) addresses the "double bind" of Black women in America who, on the one hand, are not recognized as equals in white-women led feminist movements due to their race; and on the other side, are still subject to patriarchal abuses from Black men in their homes and communities; not to mention, violently dehumanized by white men just about everywhere else (also see Collins, 1989; Collins &

Bilge, 2016; K. Crenshaw, 1989; K. W. Crenshaw, 2011). Similarly, disparities that we see in access to and experiences in technology-driven innovation markets are not only racialized but gendered as well. Most can be traced directly to the enduring legacy of patriarchal white supremacy.

Take TAF's hometown of Seattle, for example. Seattle is one of the wealthiest and fastest growing cities in the nation – a globally recognized technology innovation hub. The Duwamish Native land which Seattle sits upon is majestic; with panoramic views of snow-capped mountains, numerous stratovolcanos, glacial lakes, and verdant hills. It also boasts a modern skyline littered with the largest number of construction cranes in the nation. "The Emerald City," as it is often called, is home to global companies such as Microsoft, Amazon, Zulily, Tableau, Big Fish Games, Redfin, and Nintendo, and multiple technology districts that host offices for companies such as Twitter, Facebook, Snapchat, DropBox, and Google. In terms of demographic composition, Latinx and African American peoples in Seattle makeup just 6.6% and 7.1% of the city's population, but respectively account for 12% and 40% of its homeless population, and over 60% of nonwhite homeless people in Seattle identify as women (US Census Bureau, 2018). Again, we should take a long pause and ask ourselves and each other, how is it that over one-half of the homeless population in one of our nation's whitest, wealthiest, most technologically "innovative" cities, are nonwhite, and nonwhite women at that? What does that tell us about the structural and cultural trajectory of technology innovation in our country? Should anyone be surprised that nonwhite people, and particularly nonwhite women, are also notably absent from technology-related jobs and technology firm ownership in the region? Unsurprisingly, similar disparities are apparent when looking at health, employment, and educational outcomes – and Seattle is not alone or isolated regarding its inequitable racialized and gendered approach to innovation. Often, business and political leaders have recognized that they must do better, but do they know how? And is there enough willpower?

More importantly, what is it that needs to happen in our schools, communities, and shared public spaces to recognize what is happening, where we are as a city, and how we got here? What are the implications for educators and those who intend to do meaningful work around STEM education and social innovation? Black Feminist Theories, particularly those addressing technology and digital media, have much to offer all of us in terms considering questions such as these and providing us the tools for rigorous analysis of social inequities. The next section builds on the theoretical discussion from this section to share stories and insights from influential members of the extended TAF community, suggesting ways we all might think differently about and re-approach sociotechnical change efforts.

Part Three: Critical Conversations on Social Innovation and STEM Education

The section presents conversations from Trish Millines Dziko and three (3) influential members of the extended TAF community. The re-storied interviews outline important ideas, frameworks, or concepts that each contributor values in their work at TAF and beyond. Each conversation begins with a vignette that introduces the contributor in relation to their experiences at TAF, before delving into a more in-depth analysis of their ideas and relevant commentary from other TAF community members.

Conversations with Trish Millines Dziko

SEEDS OF A BLACK WOMAN IN TECH: THE ORIGINS OF COMMUNITY INNOVATION

Trish Millines Dziko is the Cofounder and Executive Director, of the Technology Access Foundation. This chapter explores her childhood and early life experiences that influenced her to become both a computer scientist and social entrepreneur focused on educating nonwhite students and communities. This chapter introduces connections between identity and social innovation; and provides a historical context for how TAF evolved from conception to program launch in Seattle, WA in 1996.

SNAPSHOT OF TRISH MILLINES DZIKO

Trish watched her mother start three churches in the first 17 years of her life. They lived in the small, working-class borough of Belmar, New Jersey when the struggle for Black liberation in the United States was in full swing. Trish describes growing up in the "Civil Rights Era" as a time when pride was surging through Black communities. "Black power" was palpable in art, fashions, language, and media, and persistent activism seemed to be forcing the country to rethink, and perhaps abandon, traditions of violent white supremacy. Black pride abounded radio airwaves, and artists like Donny Hathaway could be heard singing, "To be Young, Gifted, and Black." It was more than a lovely dream, for many, it was the becoming of a liberated Blackness in America – nearly

400-years in the making. Trish recounts how barriers to Black folks' full-participation in the American Dream were brought to task in courtrooms and streets, and there was hope that an end to the days of racist employment practices, legislated segregation, discriminatory housing-and-lending policies, and physical lynching had arrived. Long-overdue justice seemed within reach for many folks, even in the segregated community of Belmar. Trish's mother, a selfless and dedicated community servant, spent a lot of time supporting Belmar's Black communities through her churches. Her pride, work ethic, and orientation towards serving others left enduring impressions on a young daughter.

Trish reflected on her childhood while speaking to me at TAF headquarters in White Center (WA), her caramel-toned face lit up with beautiful energy as powerful as it is effortless. I listened as Trish told story after story of growing up in times that escaped me by 20-years. It was hard not to be inspired and infuriated. Trish is what folks call a "straight-shooter," and she does not pull punches when describing her childhood realities. I was praying the voice-recorder caught it all because I was caught-up between laughing, crying, and shaking my head, letting my notetaking surrender to her calming, low, and matter-of-fact voice. Despite growing up in an era often depicted as socio-politically adverse for Black folk, Trish offers a powerful counter-narrative:

"I was taught that I could do anything I wanted to do."

As the only child of a single mother who adopted Trish as an infant and spent much of her time struggling for earnings and serving her community, Trish understood that if she wanted something she would have to work hard to get or do, it for herself. Independence wasn't a matter of rugged individualism or a lack of concern on the part of adults in her life. It was an inherited reality due to living in a society that treated Blackness and Black womanhood with contempt and violence. Her safety necessitated that she exercised independence to navigate day-to-day life.

"There were certain places I couldn't go," Trish solemnly recalls.

Though social conditions seemed to be getting better, everything wasn't sweet. Trish recalls developing an early understanding that U.S. society was not fair for Black communities, but also witnessing adults around her model shared values for self-sufficiency and self-determination. Her hard-working mother was her most proximal example.

Regarding pivotal moments that highlight Trish's mother's direct influence on her career path as a social entrepreneur, Trish often tells the story of the day when she decided that she was not going to attend college after talking with some of her friends about what to do after high-school. In the early seventies, according to Trish, college was not an expected post-secondary pathway as it is today. There were no college-readiness programs, FAFSA, and many students were more inclined to enlist in the military or attend trade-school than enter a 4-year college, Trish recalls. Furthermore, in 1973, a person holding only a high-school diploma could expect to earn seventy-percent of what a college graduate earned, whereas by 1990 that number decreased to sixty-percent.[3] In other words, a person with just a high school diploma has a lower standard of living today than when Trish grew up.

"Being Black meant something different then," Trish says.

Trish recalls that "Uncle Johnny" had attended nearby Monmouth College on a G.I. Bill after serving in the Army. There was a firm expectation that she would find her way to college as well. It took Trish some time to build up the courage to relay her vision of bypassing college to her mother, but upon confessing her mother did not object as she expected. Instead, her mother just made Trish accompany her to work the whole summer cleaning the houses of white families in the affluent communities of Sea Girt and Spring Lake. On her first day, Trish scrubbed floors and toilets, did laundry, and got a firsthand look at the physical and affective labor her mother endured each day. The lesson was clear. A college education was not only a pathway to knowledge and employment, but there was also a nuanced sociopolitical value attached to it related to the ongoing struggle for Black liberty and social equality. In recounting the story, Trish's tone slightly rises, and her arms

---

[3] Source: U.S. Census Bureau, Current Population Survey, Annual Social and Economic Supplements.

cross over her chest as she seems to relive the tense lesson while reflecting on her childhood.

> "When white women were fighting for the right to work, Black women were already working...for free."

Trish's comment echoes renown scholar and feminist theorist, bell hooks (2000), who discusses how the feminist movement was polarized from the start because white women demanded solidarity from Black women but never saw or treated them as full equals. Black women in those days, says Trish, were still primarily relegated to the most menial work, and often cleaned white women's homes and took care of their children to provide for their own. Up until the first day of working with her mom, the gravity of socioeconomic disparities due to race and gender had primarily been invisible to a young Trish. After one day of performing labor that was common for many Black women at that time, the big picture quickly came into focus. Trish now understood the value and promise of a college education.

When asked about how she first developed a passion for technology and science, Trish is not ashamed—she grew up a nerd!

> "I was a bit odd. I had a crazy ass imagination."

Time alone and an overactive imagination meant that fear was never part of the equation when trying new things. Unguided experimentation and risk-taking were normative. When you listen to Trish describe her younger self, rummaging through her mother's cosmetics to create "powdery, perfume formulas," it conjures images of Madame C.J. Walker; a Black entrepreneur often credited as being the first woman in the United States to become a self-made millionaire. Walker, born in 1867, is often remembered as an early American philanthropist. She worked hard to elevate her community through the support of scholarships and sizable investments in educational opportunities for Black students. Trish, born almost 90 years later to the date, easily fits the mold of Walker's philanthropic tradition. However, Trish's fortunes would not come from emollients and hair-care, but kilobytes and code. When she wasn't under the bathroom sink mixing witch hazel and lotions, Trish was taking apart everything in the house that had a screw or circuit. One of her craziest ideas was trying to develop camera film using T.V. light. She failed. Guess what happened when she tried to install a radio in her new car? She somehow managed to take out the ignition—another failure.

Trish laughs about it, "*I didn't have the benefit of the Internet. I broke more stuff than I ever fixed.*"

There is a youthful excitement that comes through her voice when she relives those early moments of experimentation. "I short-circuited our house so many times," she chuckles. According to her logic, mistakes happen more often when you don't have siblings or parents who can teach you technical things. You experiment, you fail, and you learn. Her point also underscores the value of having caregivers and close social ties that can facilitate learning and access to technical information.

What Trish did have, however, was Black teachers, Black doctors, and a community of Black professionals who were actively engaged and influential in the early development of her identity as a technical problem-solver. From early childhood, it was not a reach for her to think of herself as a mathematician and computer scientist. She recalls the names of her hometown role-models with reverence and enthusiasm in her voice suggesting she positively identifies with them. Positive STEM role-models increase the likelihood that students will pursue STEM majors and careers (Davis, 1996; Palmer, Maramba, & Gasman, 2013; Weber, 2011a). Not surprisingly, childhood identification with multiple STEM role-models was a theme that emerged from each of our contributors to the book.

Belmar was a segregated town, but by the time Trish started kindergarten the K-8 system was integrated. Asbury Park High School took students from five feeder schools including hers, so they had a diverse mixture of Latino, Black, White, and Asian families. Attending Asbury changed how Trish navigated: who she sat with, who she ate with, and how she formed friendships and values. She felt the adults had more issues with the idea of integration than students did. Trish recalls social customs and unwritten community policies that dictated when and where Black youth could travel. Schools had integrated, neighborhoods had not.

For the most part, students seemed to be okay with integration according to Trish. It was the adults who did not want their kids interacting with nonwhite students, especially Black students because white parents feared their children might date them. Trish shakes her head thinking about the ridiculousness of it all, "We didn't have any interracial couples." While interracial dating was taboo, Trish enjoyed having a diverse group of friends at school. The relationships may have been a bit stilted by today's standards: until Trish's junior year of high school, there was no visiting at each other's homes and meeting up outside of school had limitations. Nonetheless, Trish enjoyed her integrated school experience and credited the experience with her being able to work well with diverse groups later in life.

Her coursework and accomplishments in the classroom almost rivaled her grit on the basketball court where she fashioned her game after then Knick's superstar guard, Earl "The Pearl" Monroe.

"*I had the spin move and all,*" Trish told me laughingly as she mimicked a pivot. Her jovial tone and animated body language suggest she still has zeal for the game. As she reflected on her childhood memories, she noted that three-years prior to her senior year, the United States Congress had passed the "Education Amendments of 1972" which included Title IX – a provision that "no persons in the United States on the basis of sex" be prohibited from participation in programs that received federal funds. Among many other things, this legislation opened opportunities for women to participate in, and receive scholarships for, collegiate athletics. Her senior year, Trish had helped lead the Asbury Park High girls' basketball team to the 1975 state championship, and her prowess on the court would help her make history. As a silky-smooth shooting guard, Trish would eventually become the first woman to earn a full ride basketball scholarship to Monmouth College (now Monmouth University), where she would go on to major in the then-nascent field of computer science. Her scholarship was a significant boost. In 1975, a college education was relatively affordable by today's standards, yet still, the cost would have been prohibitive for Trish and her family. Furthermore, in what might have been the most challenging moment in her life, Trish's mother would pass away just before her high school graduation. It was a traumatic moment that might derail many people or at least make them press pause, but with support from family, most notably her Aunt Lou, and a full-ride scholarship in hand, Trish persevered through graduation and enrolled in Monmouth as a student-athlete as planned.

At Monmouth, Trish's deep appreciation for technology blossomed. She initially intended to major in Electrical Engineering, building on her childhood passion for hacking and splicing electronic components. When asked about her motivations for her major, Trish revealed that back in high school, she had a summer job in a factory that made "bootleg" 8-track tapes of hits from the 60's and "Soul Tunes." The unauthorized productions required working hands-on with recording tapes to remove and put them on reels, and splice together mixes. A moment into the story, she admits that though she wanted to become one, she never actually reached her goal of being a "splicer.", but she learned quite a bit about the machinery. It was nonetheless a dream summer gig that combined two of Trish's passions: technology and soul music. Her summer experience, when coupled with her prior technological escapades as a youth, made electrical engineering a logical and accessible choice by the time she entered Monmouth. Hands-on experience in meaningful informal STEM learning activities supports Black girls to pursue STEM majors in college (Hill, Corbett, & Rose, 2010; Palmer et al., 2013; Weber, 2011a). As fate would have it, however, the time-schedule for electrical engineering courses conflicted with basketball practice. To stay on scholarship, Trish switched her major to computer science – a field that had undergone a dramatic facelift from being one where women thrived in WWII to one that was thoroughly dominated by white men by the mid-1970s (Abbate, 2012). That meant Trish was one of the relatively few women majoring in Computer Science (CS), but even more of an outlier because she was a Black woman. Switching majors would prove to be nearly providential, as self-determination instilled by her mother and her identification with STEM topics propelled Trish to excel in CS. Eventually, upon college graduation, Trish took an entrepreneurial risk to leave New Jersey and head to the West Coast where the technology industry was beginning to make a seismic shift.

> "Nobody knew coming out of college what they needed to know to do their jobs. The field was so young. They hired on potential mostly," Trish recalled as she reflected on her earliest employment experiences."

In Trish's experience, the technology industry was and remains dominated by a culture which tends to hold racial identity, more than anything else, as an indicator of capability. She has witnessed, first as a job candidate, then later as a program and diversity manager, how people's biases about who does and who does not have potential to succeed in tech play an overwhelming role in employment practices and access to opportunity. It was back then that she began to question, how do we explain the marked absence of talented people of color in the tech field if everyone is being hired on potential? In our conversation, she told me that technology opportunities are inherently speculative, meaning whether it's a new-hire or startup venture, there are risks involved for companies and firms to invest their precious resources in new people and projects. Risk-mitigation is a normative function and underlying logic for business and organizational managers and decision-makers (Almirall et al., 2014; Karabey, 2012; Oster, 1995). However, critical analysis of the white-male dominated U.S. tech industry suggests perceptions of "risk" are highly subjective and often consistent with patterns of systemic racism toward nonwhite groups. These patterns of "risk avoidance" are often merely metastasized biases and beliefs around race and gender that are closely linked to mainstream narratives and imaginary that rationalize systemic discrimination against nonwhite groups. Mainstream culture deals out opportunities and reifies racial exclusivity in tech communities based on peoples' proximity to established "safe" personas constructed on class, racial and gender stereotypes – namely, a college-educated "nerdy" white male. In other words, the closer a person is to reflecting the identity (e.g., behaviors, values, relationships, and aesthetics) of the dominant white-male nerd stereotype, the easier it is for decision-makers to justify taking a risk on them. Black women and other nonwhite peoples face an uphill battle in overcoming both sociocultural and structural barriers to their participation in the broader technology ecosystem. There is also a double-standard in the perception of risk because of highly publicized mainstream narratives of white "college drop-outs" such as Bill Gates and Mark Zuckerberg. These narratives make it easier to imagine white males as being able to overcome the requirement of needing a college education to succeed, but the same benefit of the doubt is not typically extended for nonwhite candidates because there are not popularized narratives to support the leap. Indeed, most folks would be hard-pressed to name a nonwhite counterpart to Bill Gates, Steve Jobs, or Zuckerberg so far as a celebrated, high-profile, technology executive, let alone one without college education. The gap in knowledge around viable counternarratives to support perceptual "risk-taking" on nonwhite candidates adds texture to the stagnant patterns in hiring, funding, and overall representation in STEM-related fields.

IDENTITY INFORMS SOCIAL INNOVATION

After brief stints in Moorestown (NJ), Tucson (AZ) and San Francisco (CA), Trish moved to Seattle in 1985 and landed a job at a small, telecommunications technology firm as their first manager of quality assurance. When she wasn't directly proving herself through her technical work and contributions, Trish spent time volunteering to teach youth near her home in Seattle's historic Central District. It is not uncommon for volunteer experiences to evolve into either full-time work or business opportunities. Many social entrepreneurs start as volunteers trying to help others solve a problem before they develop a crucial insight or reach a critical frustration point with the status quo that motivates them to initiate a solution. The causes we volunteer toward are often linked to our identities and lived experiences (Grönlund, 2011). According to the U.S. Bureau of Labor (2015), roughly 29% of Black women in the U.S. volunteered in 2015 which led all subgroups in the nation. It is necessary to recognize that Black women have consistently been at the forefront of volunteering physical, cognitive, and affective labor to build our communities, including leading progressive Black education and political initiatives to combat patriarchal white supremacy. Trish's volunteer focus was teaching students how to program computers and illuminating pathways for them to access internships and opportunities at local technology companies—a step that she optimistically thought would prevent economic disparities that plagued previous generations from extending into the dawning digital era.

In *Self-Taught*, Heather Andrea Williams (2007) chronicles the history of how Black communities in the United States have worked toward goals of literacy and education in pursuit of spiritual, political, and economic empowerment. Dating back to the times of slavery, Black women in the United States have been integral members of the Black "intelligence network" employed in a range of ways of doing-and-knowing in service of our communities (Williams, 2007). Williams (2007) describes how Black women have provided physical and emotional labor in direct opposition of white patriarchal systems of oppression, dating back to when Black women would risk eavesdropping on "master's" kitchen conversations to inform the community of political affairs, and organize clandestine literacy communities among enslaved Africans. In this way, Black women have been catalyst for epistemic shifts in what and how our communities know. Annette Henry describes *Black Feminist Pedagogy* as the living and continuous evolution of Black liberatory educational traditions which center the epistemologies and experiences of Black women (Watkins, 2005). Whereas in early U.S. history, many Black women innovators and educators' efforts primarily focused on increasing literacy so that Black people could achieve fuller political and religious lives, Trish's vision in 1996 was around the idea of increasing computer literacy so that Black and Brown communities could equitably participate in the growing tech economy. The indirect goal was Trish wanted our communities to have better influence over power, economics, and politics within our own communities.

In listening to Trish and reflecting on my time with her, I find the fact that Trish rooted her vision for TAF in her identity and experiences as a Black woman compelling. This revelation supports the idea of TAF as a relevant site for exploring Black Feminist Thought, Critical Pedagogy, and their real and potential relationships to social innovation. My experiences and work on this project suggest there is also an underappreciated connection between the experiences of Black women and the specific types of educational and social innovations they bring forward based on their skills and voices.

SEATTLE DOT COM – A UNIQUE MOMENT AND PLACE

In 1996, the time of TAF's launch, the Central District of Seattle was a unique place. Middle-class Black families owned craftsman homes on the hillsides of luxurious greenbelts that overlooked pristine lakes and snow-capped mountains. Near Trish's home in the Leschi neighborhood of the Central District, you had a three-generation household, a local reverend, a bus-driver fresh from California, and one of the original Tuskegee Airmen all living on the same block. Most residents arrived at Seattle as part of the Great Migration that relocated over 6 million Black people to northern U.S. cities from the south. Numerous Black small businesses were thriving up and down the arterials of 23rd Avenue, Rainier Avenue, Union Street, and Empire (now named Rev. Dr. Martin Luther King Jr.) Way. Despite ongoing systemic challenges to equitable participation in the broader Seattle economy, Black families in the Central District comprised a significant and visible part of the broader Seattle community. Describing her early volunteer efforts and transition into her fulltime work to launch TAF, Trish commented:

> "The CD I knew was the CD that everybody else knew way back. Mostly Black. Somewhere between medium and low-income, and that went all the way from the CD down to Rainier Beach."

The Kwanzaa principle of *Ujamma*, cooperative economics, seemed to be present in the way Central District residents patronized everything from Black barbers and salons, to Black accountants and lawyers. To some extent, the vibe was reminiscent of Trish's upbringing in Belmar which made the Central District feel like home. Like her mother before her, Trish held a core commitment to empowering others through community service, and she looked for an outlet.

Her next employment stop would be a springboard to

taking her commitment to nonwhite communities to the next level. In 1988, Trish took a job with an upstart company in Redmond, WA named Microsoft. Trish first worked as a technical program manager but soon changed her career to identify and recruit diverse candidates for technical positions at Microsoft. This role allowed her to build her network more broadly within and outside of the fast-growing Microsoft organization. It is hard to imagine, but back then, according to Trish, Microsoft's small-scale and culture promoted moving business ideas quickly from wherever they originated to executive leadership. Trish met with top executives and had a network that reached far across the organization and connected her to people who would become central to her later work as TAF's co-founder.

Nearly a decade later, as her Microsoft career flourished, Trish often contemplated her connections to industry and community – and she wondered how she might better serve the needs of young nonwhite students in the Central District and neighborhoods like it. She had volunteered to teach Visual Basic to students at the local YMCA at a lab donated by a Microsoft executive. She eventually would meet a friend and mentor who invited her to volunteer to teach C programming to students at Rainier Beach High School in south Seattle.

"I knew the CD and Rainier Beach, but I didn't know of anything in between," Trish stated as she tightened her lips to express the sharp focus she had on her work, home, and community. Trish continued with her volunteer work with her mentor and deepened her commitment to providing equitable access to technology education.

On the personal side of things, in the same year, Trish met her partner and future TAF co-founder, Jill Hull Dziko, who was a social worker. Amongst many other things, Jill and Trish shared a concern for students and education. Jill had clients who were in middle school and had a designation of having behavioral disorders. During Jill's visits to their classroom, however, she noticed many teachers did not engage with the students. Jill witnessed students not getting the education they deserved, and she felt little was being done to acknowledge or remedy the problem in a meaningful way. In a conversation with Jill, she vividly recalled the classroom scenes and racialized disparities, especially for Black boys:

> *"They were immediately shuffled off into this pathway that a lot of times defined the rest of their life for them because the assumption was they couldn't learn, and they were told they couldn't learn."*

One day Jill brought a group of her students over to Microsoft to visit the high school interns where Trish was running the program.

"*Lightbulbs just went off for her students,*" recalls Trish.

Faces lit up, both groups of students bonded with each other, and many of the visiting students made a connection between the environment they were in and young people like themselves they saw in it. That was also the "aha" moment for Trish. Trish and Jill saw an opportunity. For them, it wasn't about filling gaps in the educational system or merely working toward saving students from the "digital divide." Instead, they saw tremendous untapped potential in the very students who lived in their community. They felt together they could create a program that capitalized on students' brilliance, energy, and seemingly innate curiosity for technology.

In 1995, near the height of the dot.com era, Trish got the opportunity to retire from Microsoft as did many of her workplace peers who shared in the company's explosive growth. Suddenly, a new class of wealthy individuals in Seattle commonly called the 'Microsoft Millionaires' were born. These relatively young, mostly thirty-somethings, suddenly found themselves privileged to retire early, buy newer, bigger homes, launch startups, and for some, launch their visions for changing the world. Trish had become part of a cohort of elite influencers in the regional technology scene who were politically and economically leveraged to make moves, quickly. The following year in 1996, Trish and Jill both decided to leave their full-time jobs to launch the Technology Access Foundation (TAF).

TAF: DIVIDES, GAPS, AND OPPORTUNITIES

Trish and Jill seeded the TAF's launch with $150K their own money and would continue to contribute funds over the first five years of operation. As with any entrepreneurial venture, one of Trish and Jill's first big tasks was forming a trusted group of advisors and potential board members. Neither had much experience with nonprofit management and they wanted to make sure that their communities were part of the process for vetting their ideas and intentions.

"*I didn't know anything about running a board,*" Trish self-deprecatingly laughed.

Trish and Jill's relative inexperience in the nonprofit domain is significant because it underscores a common progression whereby many social entrepreneurs move from the for-profit to the nonprofit sector to realize their social-change vision. It is worthwhile to ask how was the decision to structure TAF as a nonprofit reached, and what, if any, possible alternative structures for pursuing TAF's work did they considered? In *"Strategic Management of Nonprofit Organizations,"* Sharon Oster (1995), discusses how the nonprofit space exists between industry and government to provide services to the public that might be overreaching or impractical for a government to provide directly, but yet not commercially attractive enough to entice profit-driven entrepreneurs or capital investment. Another way to look at it is this: nonprofits have tended to do what government cannot, will not, or should not do, and those with capital cannot, will not, or should not invest in – normally because it is either unprofitable, unpragmatic, or unpopular. Nonprofits often operate around gaps in services that government and industry value but cannot directly provide or scale to the public. Nonprofits are thus a decentralized sociopolitical structure that, in part, derive their power from being relevant to acknowledged gaps between industry and government. These gaps result from direct and indirect, power-laden negotiations between elected officials, industry, researchers, and meaning-making institutions (e.g., news media, schools, pro-sports) that engage the broader public. Jill touched on this in her commentary when describing their motivations for founding TAF, and offering a critique of government and society stating:

> "*TAF is innovation, but it's innovation almost that shouldn't be.*"

As part of her critique, Jill explained that she feels the conditions nonwhite students face should not exist because ideally, we should have moved past racialized oppression. Her sentiment was echoed by an early TAF Staff member who in describing their connection to TAF's mission, identified as "white" and "male" and stated:

> "*I want to fight sometimes when I hear about how people get treated in the tech industry, and how women and people of color – even when they get recruited – aren't made to feel welcome.*"

The same staff member described their feeling of wanting to persuade other white adults to think more in alignment with TAF's values and mission but confessed that they felt their time was better spent working directly with nonwhite students. The message they worked to impart to students regarding navigating the technology industry is:

> "*I want you here. I want you there in that mix even though it's going to be difficult and people may not support you like I would want to support you.*"

The value of TAF's mission to early parents and caretakers is clear too. Several parents spoke of TAF offering a service that in many ways was hard for them to properly value in 1996 because nobody knew how much computing technology would impact society. Most adults just knew it was important. When asked how they value their child's TAF experience now, a parent responded:

> "*Giving young people access to the tools that they would need to not only survive but to thrive in what was before them in a world that was fast moving to being largely and solely dependent upon technology…a lot of them didn't have computers in their home. I'd have to say as a parent it's just really valuing the fact that there was something that could come into the lives of my children that I knew I could not provide for them myself.*"

Staff identities are a big part of TAF's success and play a vital role in the organizational culture. TAF has consistently had a predominately nonwhite executive team and staff which is mainly due to an operating principle that TAF strives to hire from inside the communities and families that it serves – a good practice. Speaking on the value of being in a mostly nonwhite organization, a current staff member that identifies as white stated:

> *"It definitely adds integrity to the work in a way that isn't guaranteed. Not that you couldn't do good work in other ways with other staffing demographics, but I do think it's really important. So, for one, I think there's a different kind of understanding of the experiences of students of color."*

Though Trish's path is relatively unique, she is not alone. Countless Black women across our communities and country have persevered through adverse contexts that would break the backs of many folks who are riding the silent waves of racial and patriarchal privilege. Among those Black women, is Dr. Sheila Edwards-Lange, President of Seattle Central College, and one of Trish's contemporaries whose work has supported thousands of nonwhite students to access higher education. Keisha Scarlett is a former Washington State Principal of the Year, and currently serves as Executive Director of Organizational Development & Equity for Seattle Public Schools. In a TAF podcast episode featuring the three of them (available on iTunes and Soundcloud), they spoke of the traumatic costs of affective labor that Black women burden in service of their communities and society – with their contributions often unsung or minimized.

Trish's childhood and early career narratives highlight a range of issues that are central to understanding and solving problems that face many nonwhite communities in the United States while centering experiences common to many Black women. An important question we might ask is, who has the lived experiences and knowledge that might best prepare them to deliver value and provide solutions that will positively impact nonwhite communities? So long as white-maleness is the *de facto* proxy for technology readiness, and "model minority" stereotypes prevail as the mainstream exception to the rule, we can expect continued stagnation in both diversity numbers for tech companies and investment in nonwhite entrepreneurship and social innovation.

Conversations with Dr. Nicole M. Joseph

NOBODY I CAN'T TEACH: UNDERSTANDING CRITICAL RACE THEORY AND CRITICAL PEDAGOGY

Few people have contributed to the success of TAF's work with students as much as Dr. Nicole M. Joseph. Before her current role as an Assistant Professor of mathematics and science education in the department of Teaching and Learning at Vanderbilt University, Dr. Joseph worked with TAF as the inaugural Math Instructional Coach on the Education Team tasked with designing the TAF Academy approach to STEM project-based learning. Her passion for "Black and Brown" students is radiant and as is her commitment to working with teachers to develop a critical conscientiousness around their teaching practices and classrooms. In any environment, Dr. Joseph raises the level of student and adult discourse beyond mainstream tropes and clichés which tend to focus on student achievement and equity, toward a more critical conversation about power relationships, identity, systemic oppression, and pedagogical integrity. For five (5) years her presence was a pillar of the TAF Academy teaching and learning community, and today her work as a researcher continues to inform TAF and countless educators across the globe. In this chapter, we introduce Dr. Joseph and highlight some of the ideas and experiences she shared that have contributed to her identity and professional work as a math and science educator, critical *theorist, and researcher.*

SNAPSHOT OF DR. NICOLE M. JOSEPH

One word describes institutional systems and actors that perpetuate gender racism in math, "Raggedy!"

It is a word Dr. Nicole M. Joseph, an Assistant Professor of Mathematics and Science Education at Vanderbilt University, uses with humor and nuance. She laments the raggedy schools, teaching practices, and learning conditions that research shows turn many "Black and Brown" students away from mathematics by the time they hit middle school. It's a national trend that she is committed to changing through her work and research—particularly for Black girls who experience unique forms of oppression at the intersection of patriarchy and white supremacy, which is called *gender racism*.

"*I do care about all students, but I have a particular love for Black students and oppressed groups in our society,*" Dr. Joseph proclaims.

> "It is important for me to contribute research that centers such students to tell a complete story of their experiences, which should [consider] the historical, political, and social issues that have shaped their experiences. Much of the research about Black students is from a deficit perspective and devoid of contextualization. So, for example, when we

> read about Black students being at the bottom of the mathematics performance hierarchy, explanations should move beyond those that blame the students and should include how and in what ways our educational systems have negatively shaped Black students' opportunities to learn mathematics."

She explains to me that her love for Black students stems from her own identity and lived-experiences as a Black woman who grew up and then worked as a public educator in Seattle.

> "I grew up in Seattle, went through public schools: Washington Middle School, Cleveland High School. Right there in the city! Part of my life, I grew up in the projects in Yesler Terrace. And then we moved over into the Mount Baker area in South Seattle."

Even over the phone from her current home of Nashville, Dr. Joseph's voice conjured memories of Seattle's largely gentrified core and displaced Central District community. There is a bittersweet tone in each of her references that memorializes the loss of Black space. Many of her memories were neighborhoods, schools, streets, and former housing projects and communities that were gentrified by regional growth. She values the role of history in education in communities like the Central District and South End of Seattle. Dr. Joseph explains:

> "Because I'm a historian, I think about when a teacher is

> *thinking about what impacts learning; they have to understand sociocultural and economic factors. They also need to understand historically, what have been historical circumstances that affect the education of students and particularly oppressed marginalized students. [For example] African American students' education in this country has been significantly impacted and affected by policies and practices written to prevent and dismantle Black community."*

Dr. Richard Morrill, Geography Professor at the University of Washington, traced the history of Seattle's Central District over eighty years, from 1930 to 2010, to show factors that contributed to how Black communities grew substantially through the 80s and then sharply declined due to displacement and gentrification (Morrill, 2013). Morrill (2013) notes that racialized discrimination against Black and nonwhite families was the dominant factor that influenced the creation of segregated low and middle-class communities in Central and South Seattle through the early 1980's. Dr. Joseph explains how the history of discrimination affected public education in Seattle's Black communities and many more like them:

> *"Before segregation, Black people went to segregated schools and had Black teachers and only some were white. Those [Black] teachers were committed to change and disrupting the discourse around Black students being*

inferior and less than [whites]. Once Brown vs. Board happened, a lot of those teachers lost their jobs, Black students integrated, and they moved students, but they didn't deal with the context of having teachers who didn't care for Black students in their schools. Today we still see remnants and sometimes the same things as we've gone through re-segregation and gentrification – and all of that impacts oppressed communities."

By the 1990s, Seattle's ascension as a technology-hub spurred the growth of the downtown area which made the nearby Central District attractive for settlement by waves of arriving professionals to the growing tech ecosystem. The "settlers" were typically white, well-schooled, and arriving from other parts of the United States (Morrill, 2013). Among other things, the settlers bought homes in undervalued communities which prompted increased taxes, and populations were displaced. Contemporary scholars of the logics, politics, and practices of *settler colonialism* note that settler expansion necessitates the destruction of Indigenous communities for the creation of new settlements that reify and extend settler privilege (Snelgrove, Dhamoon, & Corntassel, 2014; Wolfe, 2006). Recently, the term *neo-indigenous* has been used by educators in the United States to "connect groups of people based on their shared experience" such as those racialized as Black who live in urban populations with Native Nations, "Aboriginals" and Indigenous peoples (Emdin, 2016). Though the use of the term by educators is often well-intended and meant to express solidarity between oppressed groups, I reject it because it harms and obfuscates the real struggles of Indigenous and Native Nations to sustain their sovereignty, spiritual and epistemic traditions, and recover their homelands. For example, Africans were brought to the United States as free labor to transform "terra" into white settler property and wealth (Jackson, 2014). Accordingly, "Black" communities such as the Central District that sprang forth from the enslavement experience were unequivocally subordinate to the larger project of settler colonialism. Notable exceptions include several Black communities that sought to establish Black independence on their terms in collaboration and solidarity with Native Nations and Indigenous peoples including Black nationalist organizations that had philosophies of repatriation. Although far more common Black peoples in the United States made use of Native land for their own purposes of Black economic stability and assimilation into the United States mainstream; making them tributaries, albeit segregated ones, to the larger project of expanding white settler colonialism (Jackson, 2012). It is a harsh but accurate reality to which many Black people in decolonizing efforts are now awakening, as they are to the reality that several Native Nations bought and sold enslaved Africans (see Krauthamer, 2013). Thus, in the U.S., the histories and experiences of Black, Native, and Indigenous peoples are entangled, but different. Rather than commit the error of mislabeling or conflating various colonized peoples' experiences, it is more accurate to openly recognize that there is a consistent logical and behavioral pattern exercised by those who enter spaces as settler colonialists, and another by those colonized. Dr. Joseph believes teachers need *critical pedagogical content-knowledge* around nuances such as how do we categorize and discuss the experiences of oppressed populations in ways that are conscientious and emancipatory:

> *"We need teachers that are much more radical. We need teachers who care about students, and I'm not talking about the soft and fuzzy care. The type of care that Paulo Freire or bell hooks would suggest which is conscientious. How do we [develop] teachers that care about raising the consciousness of students to engage in deep learning for change and liberation?"*

Liberation of the oppressed must be the aim of education, according to Dr. Joseph. Settler colonial patterns in the U.S. adversely affect Indigenous and "other groups" including Black communities because an underlying logic is the supremacy of "whiteness" that entitles those racialized as white to assert economic, epistemological, and political superiority overs those categorized as nonwhite, without consideration of the will of colonized populations (Jackson, 2014; Smith, 1999; Tuck & Yang, 2012; Wolfe, 2006). Though Indigenous, Black, and Latinx groups have distinct and entangled histories, another common experience is that all have had racialized education programs instituted to facilitate their colonization. These programs have included the removal of Native children from their families, formal curricula that reinforces the supremacy of whiteness, and policies that subvert colonized communities' efforts to be self-determined in setting educational agendas for their communities (Grande, 2015; Watkins, 2001). Though an extended discussion of settler colonial logics, politics and practices is beyond the scope of this book, it is essential to contextually note that the Central District of Seattle and many similar communities nationwide are relevant sites for understanding the entanglement of Black communities, Indigenous peoples, and white-settler histories. These histories and related narratives have indispensable significance to any meaningful effort around education.

RACE, GENDER, AND EDUCATION

For Dr. Joseph, her identity as a Black woman has provided her firsthand invaluable experiences with anti-blackness, patriarchy, and white supremacy, as both student and educator in Seattle, and now a professor and math education researcher at Vanderbilt University.

> "Being a Black woman educator in the United States, which is a very racist, sexist and homophobic place, I get the opportunity to speak for those that do not, cannot, or will not speak for themselves. And when I say speak for, I mean in a way that is co-constructed. So [my focus is] how do I help my students develop a voice for themselves to

transform their broader life outcomes."

Research studies show that Black girls routinely experience gender racism as a normative part of their public education experiences including from teachers and peers who have low expectations of them and doubt their capability to engage in rigorous work (Grossman & Porche, 2014; Joseph, Hailu, & Boston, 2017; Joseph et al., 2016). In our conversation for the "This Is the Work Podcast," Dr. Joseph shared one childhood story of how her mother once stood stealthily at the doorway of her classroom to ensure that she was receiving proper instruction. When Nicole's mother observed that her daughter was not challenged, she advocated that Nicole move to in higher-level coursework. Dr. Joseph recalls then meeting a new elementary teacher who encouraged her in math-and-science and indulged her predisposition to question everything twice. In Chapter One of this book, TAF Co-founder, Trish Millines Dziko, shared a similar experience of being improperly "tracked" in math as a young Black girl. A former TAF Parent echoed Nicole's experience while sharing her reflections on her three Black daughters' experiences in school:

> *"I discovered nice girls get that halo effect and get less attention, right? Academically, you get, 'Oh, they're nice. They know how to raise their hands. They know how to sit quietly. They know how to blah blah blah', but there were things that they did not understand because they*

didn't get the attention."

Gender racism perpetuates through continuous social proliferation of negative stereotypes, biases, and beliefs about Black women, which at their core, aim to privilege whiteness and maleness (hooks, 1981). Mainstream media and the Internet are powerful mechanisms through which society constructs and receives messages about Black women, which tend toward anti-black and patriarchal perspectives and values (hooks, 2000; Noble, 2018). A predominantly white (>90%) teaching workforce absorbs these messages and brings them into classrooms where they are entrusted to teach young Black women. In Dr. Joseph's forthcoming book, *Mathematizing Feminism: Black Girls' and Women's Experiences in the P-20 Mathematics Pipelines,* she illuminates how these negative mainstream messages about and perceptions of Black women contribute to the systemic lack of attention and support for them to engage in rigorous STEM coursework in their P-20 experiences (Joseph, n.d.). She was witnessed that absent direct, often personalized advocacy for their inclusion and access to rigorous learning opportunities, it more likely that Black girls and women will get bypassed for opportunities that lead to STEM college majors and professions. Black women are also among those least likely to find STEM mentors, be recommended for STEM majors and opportunities, and recruited into STEM tech companies (Beasley, 2011; Grossman & Porche, 2014; Palmer et al., 2013; Weber, 2011b). At the far end of the pipeline, Black women are unsurprisingly among those least likely to be funded for STEM entrepreneurship (Dorsey, 2016; Finnery & Rencher, 2016). The onslaught of inequities faced by Black women such as Dr. Joseph, Trish, and countless Black girls in our classroom, underscore the value of leveraging Black feminist pedagogy to center the lived-experiences and voices of Black women to improve educational and social outcomes for Black women and other oppressed groups.

PATHWAYS TO CRITICAL SCHOLARSHIP

After a young Dr. Joseph graduated from Seattle University with undergraduate degrees in business economics and mathematics; a pivotal moment came when a mentor, Dr. Zakia Stewart, encouraged her to accept a post within a community of progressive Black educators at Zion Preparatory Academy [defunct]. Dr. Joseph credits her early-career peers at Zion and the professional learning community they co-created for pushing her towards scholarly research on human development and critical studies. In our conversations with her, she routinely references the works of notable scholars such as Patricia Hill Collins, bell hooks, Derrick Bell, Paulo Freire, Geneva Gay, and her doctoral advisor at the University of Washington, renown multicultural educator, James A. Banks. Emancipatory scholar-activism is a core value situated deep within her DNA, and as a mathematician and historian, Dr. Joseph values it for its ability to provide inspirational counter-narratives to stigmas, myths, and stereotypes about Black and Brown students in math.

> "Audre Lorde, Martin Luther King, Malcolm X and all of these incredible intellectuals and on the ground scholars that came before us are folks that I often draw upon when I do get weary."

With each breath, the same deep satisfaction Dr. Joseph's feels about math radiates from her spirit when discussing her critical scholarship and work with teachers. Her philosophy on instructional coaching is anchored in a belief that it is necessary to "cheer and challenge" teachers to do their best work in an equitable way that values each student for who they are. Even her most critical analysis of public education has a vein of enthusiasm as she discusses challenges that teaching-colleges face in preparing adults, the majority of whom are white and not embedded in Black and Brown communities, to provide rigorous, relevant connections to the worlds of mathematics for students.

As a teacher and instructional coach, Dr. Joseph has worked with hundreds of students and scores of teachers around Seattle to recognize and overcome systemic oppression in the educational process, leveraging *Critical Race Theory* as a pillar of her praxis.

> "An instructional coach is someone who is a thinking partner with a teacher to help them reflect on how to get better at teaching."

For disambiguation, *Critical Theory* is an area of philosophy that examines social phenomena from the standpoint of interrogating how power is distributed and performed, often along the lines of race, class, gender, and ability. Power, in this case, can be defined in terms of personal or communal agency and is closely related to the concept of self-determination, or the freedom for a person or community to pursue its own best interest without undue influence or constraint. Critical Theory invites questions such as, "What is the political context?", "Who are the actors?", "How is power distributed among them?", "How are political relationships performed and maintained?" and "What roles do various ideologies and institutional structures play?" Critical Race Theory is a perspective within Critical Theory that holds the construction of race and the project of white supremacy is central to any analysis of power in society. The foundations and central ideas of Critical Theory are expounded at length by prominent scholars including Audre Lorde, bell hooks, Patricia Hill Collins, Derrick Bell, Paulo Freire, Frantz Fanon, Eduardo Bonilla-Silva, and contemporaries of Dr. Joseph such as Kimberly Crenshaw, Carla Shedd, Safiya Noble, Ibram Kendi, and Crystal Fleming.

Getting better does not happen in a vacuum, and many courageous conversations must be had to move teachers in their practice. Her analysis runs parallel to Christopher Emdin (2016), Columbia University professor and author of *For White Folks Who Teach in the Hood: And the Rest of Y'all Too*. In working with predominantly white teachers in urban environments, Emdin (2016) found that teachers often bring "fear-based" narrative, biases and dispositions towards students into the classroom that limit them from making meaningful connections to students and their work. . They hold deep deficit perspectives and persist and are challenging to (Joseph, Jett, & Leonard, 2018). These fears also extend toward systems and structure that teachers must navigate to provide meaningful education to students because far too often district practices and structures are more closely tied to enduring colonial patterns of education, than they are the development of student voice and liberation. In discussing the affordances of TAF's innovation of the public-private partnership, a former TAF Academy teacher noted:

> "Teachers live in a culture of fear at a national level, and it's an epidemic. Having that public-private partnership where TAF could insulate us a bit and have those [tough] conversations about 'no, we will not do that' or 'we need some autonomy. Because I always said that if I am afraid in this profession, then I will leave it."

The word "autonomy" was a staple in our work with TAF Academy as it was with many small and progressive school near the turn of the 20th century. Autonomy was a way to describe schools and teachers' need to make informed-localized decisions for their students based on intimate knowledge of their students, families, schools, and communities. I made ensuring and protecting autonomy for the teachers and the school a top priority for TAF Academy management. Part of their autonomy was working with Dr. Joseph to help them critically look at their work and roles, so they didn't reproduce the same outcomes as a mainstream traditional public school. Dr. Joseph's experience as a critical theorist and instructional coach helped her recognize challenges with both young and experienced teachers, and then responsively move them toward a critical conscientiousness in the classroom. A former TAF Academy teacher that Dr. Joseph supported described how she valued her TAF experience, stating:

> "Being one of the few white staff members is probably one of the most valuable workplace experiences I have ever had. It is rare that you see a staff that is predominantly people of color serving students of color where the staff actually represents the population that you're serving. That is super rare not only in the nonprofit world but the education world as well, and that is something that I'm [extremrely] proud of."

White staff members at TAF are continuously challenged and supported to move beyond their privilege and work towards equitable terms. The teacher added, "We had the conversations. We didn't avoid them." Another TAF staff member added in term of speaking on their privilege as a self-identified white woman:

> "I grew up in a very like middle class white privileged space and so it wasn't really until college that I had this realization of like a lot of people don't live like I live and

there's an implication to that and I'm complicit in that."

For parents and caretakers, it makes a big difference when they see teachers as being connected to and invested in their communities beyond the school day. One parent noted speaking on Washington State's predominantly white teaching force:

> *"I'm not going to see you, you know, at my place of worship wherever that might be, right? I'm not going to see you at the public library. So, in essence, you have this outside being that comes into my life from 9-3 and then you disappear right?"*

Another TAF Staff member chimed in on how they internalized the workplace conversations on race and power and what it meant for their understanding of the TAF mission.

> *"It's always going to be a conversation as long as people think that there's a difference based on the color of your skin or your culture which for me, it can be good or bad. It's how you look at it. But I think everybody should have access to fulfill their potential as far as they can."*

There needs to be a broadening of how we see our students and their behaviors. There is research that speaks to how different students learn based on learning styles and modalities that underappreciated in many traditional public schools. TAF Academy used a project-based learning model that helped to seamlessly integrate opportunities for different types of learning, from conventional direct-instruction to constructivist and group-based project work. A TAF Academy teacher spoke on the value of project-based learning in taking a more holistic approach to work with students:

> *"It was easy for me to fit into a public school that wanted to do work around project-based learning because that's how I think kids holistically really understand all the content that you're trying to give them."*

Authentic project-based learning supports different learning styles by giving teachers and students the flexibility to connect teaching and learning to real-world projects that have value outside of school. Rather than traditional direct instruction where students "sit and get" their instruction in a model Freire (1993) described as "banking education," project-based learning uses "guiding questions" to frame learning around topics and issues that are relevant to student lives. Teachers work as facilitators of learning and inquiry instead of all-knowing "experts" who hold knowledge that gets deposited in students. Project-based learning is not easy work for teachers accustomed to traditional modes of instruction. At its core, it requires a significant reallocation of time, resources, and focus toward collaboration between teachers, students, and communities of adults beyond the classroom, from caretakers to professionals.

TAF Co-Founder Jill Dziko, commented on the educational values and how she thinks about traditional disparities in public schools:

> *"I think we need to look at it more holistically rather than just kids are here to learn for six hours, and we make them sit in their seat, and if a kid can't do that, then we see that as a behavior problem."*

Critical Race Theory and Critical Pedagogy provide educators necessary perspectives to see how white supremacy and racialized identities affect the lives and liberation of students and communities. Absent these critical perspectives of consciousness, the best of intentions tends to inadvertently reproduce and reify colonial logics, practices, and relationships, extending white supremacy and patriarchy to new generations.

TAF ACADEMY: A CRITICAL TEACHING COMMUNITY

Critical scholarship inspires us to ask questions such as, how much longer must we accept gross inequity of power and resources as a normative function of institutions in a society that espouses values of freedom, equality, and justice? And though Dr. Martin Luther King encouraged our society to recognize the "arch of history is long," we feel that those of us inclined toward a more critical view of justice should spare no effort to bring our works full throttle. Thus, increasingly, we believe it is an indispensable and urgent matter for our students, teachers, community partners, and institutional allies to develop a critical lens in classrooms, schools, and communities. We are certain that it is impossible to deeply understand and effectively support education and sociotechnical innovation that affect our communities, without first thinking critically about factors such as race, class, gender, and ability.

One of the hallmarks of TAF Academy during its nine (9) years of operation was a palpable current of critical thought and discourse that was cultivated by my collaborations with and tutelage from Dr. Joseph. Along with our colleagues, we cheered and challenged each other to question and reflect critically about race and power including our beliefs and behaviors about and toward our students. Holding a mirror up to teachers and colleagues new to this practice was a big part of establishing the TAF Academy community. When speaking about conversations they had with their peers and administration about race and class, one teacher commented:

> "So not being a person of color, it's been interesting negotiating that space where it's like 'What do you know about that?' You know 'Why do you think you can help? Why do you want to help anyway?'"

The comment shows a level of transparency and willingness for the community to engage each other in conversations about race, and to question each other's values and motivations instead of working off assumptions around how everyone arrives in the profession.

Another teacher commented on balancing the mission of STEM with the larger project of holistic education of nonwhite students:

> "It wasn't just about the technology, first and foremost. That of course was the content, but all that surrounded that had to do with the relationships [and] being able to see my Brown children as brilliant and empowering them to live in their brilliance."

A TAF Academy alumnus speaking on their experience commented:

> "I was equipped from 9th grade and 10th grade to compete as a college student by 11th grade. So, I really feel like I owe a lot of that to TAF Academy. It really fostered my abilities and my skill set and helped me to grow into the person that I am today I would say."

A TAF parent commented on the impact of TAF's culture.

> "I think if you talk to any kid who went to TAF no matter really how long they went there, they knew that no matter how long they were there, what was going on, that somebody truly cared about them and somebody wanted to put them first. Their education, their family, and them."

Today, nobody can change Dr. Joseph's mind on the fact that every Black and Brown student can learn to love mathematics. It is a core belief—an epistemological commitment—that she has held since well before her days as the inaugural Instructional Coach at TAF Academy. She continues this praxis through her research at Vanderbilt University where she investigates the math experiences of Black women and girls. She is a co-editor of Interrogating Whiteness and Relinquishing Power: White Faculty's Commitment to Racial Consciousness in the Classroom, and a forthcoming book, "Mathematizing Feminism: Black Girls' and Women's Experiences in the P-20 Mathematics Pipelines." Dr. Joseph is also the founder of the Tennessee March for Black Women in STEM, an annual awareness march that takes place in September.

Conversations with David D. Harris

HACKER IN YOUR HARD DRIVE: DESIGNING AND
HACKING EDUCATION AND SOCIAL INNOVATION

When we first committed to the act of developing this book in 2016, David D. Harris was one of the first people we requested to be a contributor. David is the Startup Advocate for the City of Seattle. He was responsible for innovation at TAF Academy as the STEM Program Manager from 2011 to 2015. David initially joined TAF under my direction where he spearheaded the launch of the Teacher-Scientist Partnership (TSP) program that brought nonwhite software development professionals into the TAF Academy classrooms to co-teach with alongside teachers. David also organized several student-centered events and learning opportunities including the first STEM Expo and several trips abroad. Beyond his work at TAF, David is a foremost thought-leader and organizer in the Seattle area. He has led several economic development efforts including the historic event, Hack the CD, which was the first hackathon in Seattle focused on addressing Black communities' access to the technology ecosystem. Recently, David partnered with entrepreneur, David Pierre-Louis, to conduct user-research for Kay Tita - a sustainable community resource organization that cultivates partnerships, raises capital, and facilitates impact investing opportunities in Port-au-Prince, Haiti. This chapter builds on several conversations with David about his work at TAF and his broader philosophies for *approaching design, innovation, and community development through education.*

SNAPSHOT OF DAVID D. HARRIS

David D. Harris does not pop his own collar. He is a rare instance of someone who is soft-spoken yet powerful; humble while highly-visible; contemplative, yet a decisive risk-taker, and a serial entrepreneur. In the greater Seattle community, David is a quiet giant. He is also a self-described "hacker" – a person who can take something designed for one thing and artfully repurpose it for another, and in doing so, derive an increased value or benefit.

When we first committed to the act of developing this book, David was one of the first people we reached out to interview. In other words, he was the resident-hacker. Speaking with David by online chat, he describes three principles of hacking: *evolution, manifestation,* and *future building*. On the first principal of hacking, evolution, David explains:

> *"Hacking takes seemingly disparate ingredients, mixes them, and creates something new. This bricolage is now reified as a thing that simultaneously existed but didn't exist previously in the same state."*

Hacking is about evolution. The ingredients David references are not just material (i.e., physical matter) but intangibles such as behavioral, spiritual, philosophical, and conceptual substances as well. David suggests the universe has its proprietary logic of evolutionary hacking, and he does not necessarily consider humans as separate from that order. In working closely with David as his "director" on the organization chart, but peer in practice, we often strategized on how to navigate stubborn institutional systems and adult mindsets within the organizations we worked. Our goal was to manifest exceptional opportunities and outcomes for our students. We used the term hacking to describe our work. Courses, content, systems, and adults needed to evolve, and we were often agents-of-change for moving things in a better direction for students and our school community. For example, one of our biggest collaborative hacks was the development of the Teacher Scientist Partnership (TSP) program which brought nonwhite technical professionals into the classrooms to teach coding at TAF Academy. This program won a 2013 Ashoka Changemakers national award for innovation. Many of the things and situations we hacked were capable of being before our interventions, but they needed a vision and catalyst. We were simply evolving them to a new state to manifest a new set of relationships (e.g., people, time, space, matter) and related outcomes. David describes "manifestation," the second principle of hacking:

> "Besides the existence of the new thing, there is also the process of how the new thing became. What started as an idea, a thought, might have merged with other ideas, and those ideas might start to take the shape of its container or constraints."

If evolution is about the transformation of something from one state to another, manifestation is about the process of transference from one state to another. In other words, evolution is *what* happens, while manifestation is about *how* things come to be. David continues:

> *"Eventually, through alchemy and action, the idea morphs into the next state of matter as a prototype, which may be the seed for the next idea and evolution."*

David uses the word "morph" which in biology and linguistics the is associate with transformation of structure and form; with *morphology* being a term that is used to describe the shapes and structure-of-relationships that makeup an organism or word, respectively. For example, human morphology refers not only to the human body (i.e., anatomy) but also to its development and its relationships to human activity. Hacking begins with thoughts or ideas, which once held by individuals or groups, begin to manifest into new states of being that inspire the next idea or evolutionary step or activity. Manifestation is about the "alchemy" that David references, which seeks to bring the idea forward in a altered state. In this way, hacking can be considered a phenomenon that has both biological and linguistic components, the former about how humans tap into the universal evolutionary logic, or code, and the latter about the manifestation of ideas and ideologies which are invariably rooted in language and words. David closes with the third principle of hacking, future building:

> *"Whether viewed as "good or bad," "white hat or black hat," after something is hacked then it will never be the same, just like we can't knowingly alter the past. In a sense, hacking is a tool to build the future - we can't go back - you can't unthink the thought."*

Mainstream discourses on hacking in the U.S. use the term "white hat" or "black hat" to describe various types of hacker behavior, where you might guess, "white" refers to ethical and "black" refers to criminal. David uses these common hacking terms to signify his awareness of how white supremacy is embedded into even the most seemingly advance dialogues in our society. He also infuses culturally relevant language to ensure I understand that he is speaking from a different lexicon and epistemology of hacking. Nonetheless, his main point is clear, which is that whether hacking results from virtuous or vicious intent, it has a permanent impact on its objects and participants.

THE ART OF HACKING EDUCATION

David notes that the current education system was not designed with nonwhite communities in mind. Thus, the current education system needs to be hacked. Before David's five-year tenure as the STEM Program Manager at TAF Academy, he spent time at Microsoft and Apple where he got exposure to mainstream hacker discourses and communities. He envisions hacking as a fundamental skill need to affect change:

"We don't do copy and paste. We do original artwork!"

His softly stated metaphor is a comparative critique of mainstream educational reform efforts. He contrasts popular education reform efforts against the work he engaged in at TAF and explains "copy and paste" as being connected to the corporate commodification of public education and artistic innovation. In *Youth Resistance Research and Theories of Change*, Tuck and Yang (2013) describe a similar phenomenon:

> *"Progressive educators, activists and researchers find our best ideas appropriated by Districts or philanthropy and turned into a mandate, a reform, more aptly a de-form: individualized, privatized, and stripped of racial justice or equity."* – (Tuck & Yang, 2013, p. 52)

In David's eyes, innovative nonwhite-led organizations like TAF are necessary because they are capable of hacking stagnant systems and providing leadership to engage others in that work. At TAF Academy, corporate and private partners are engaged in bringing forth ideas and solutions, but only under the direction and leadership of teachers and staff who made conscious decisions about who and how they would engage partners in teaching and learning. A former TAF executive compared their experience at TAF to previous work they had done in education:

Far too often, public educators face unnecessarily restrictive conditions that often stifle students and teachers from being competent and compassionate problem-solvers. The restrictions include undesirable, and often unnecessary, constraints in systems and resources that determine who, how, and under what conditions adults and students engage in teaching and learning. One of the best things about working in an organization that supports hacking are the license to circumnavigate unnecessary constraints and to leave your mark on the organization. The same former TAF executive spoke on the culture of entrepreneurship at TAF:

> "[TAF is] a place where you're able to throw ideas out there and truly pursue them, but employees also have to be able to get through the crummy parts. [Sometimes] it's hard to get to a solution. Perseverance is a [necessary] because again the work is not easy."

A former colleague spoke to us about what makes a person successful in an organization like TAF:

> "Folks have to be raring to go and take on that work and feel comfortable either on their own or that they're going to be organizing [people and things]. Your stamp in this work is evident."

David models an ethic around hacking that was contagious for those around him and evident in the ways people describe their TAF experiences. Several of the smart strategies for how TAF and TAF Academy staff affected changed came from ideas David put forward in the community and modeled in terms using them to support students. In some cases, strategies can involve humor and caretaking of adult community members even when they are wrong, but never at the expense of kids. A TAF staff member described common types of pushback they received from adults who were rigid and traditional in their behavior and thinking:

> "I've done this for 30 years. I don't want to change. You can tell me everything you want to about how it's going to help my kids but either I don't have it in me or I'm just risk-averse or I've been burned, and I don't want to go down that road again." That's where the shaming or the embarrassing them to do the right thing comes in. I'm okay with giving them a graceful way to exit."

As with most folk at TAF, then and now, and as with many other startups and non-profits, David's job was vaguely defined and grossly under-resourced. It is fair to say that David didn't just wear many hats, he was responsible for outfitting teachers and staff with them too. Staying with the metaphor, David sourced the raw materials and fabrics, developed a method for artisanship, created a business model, and even performed marketing and retail! The bounds of David's hat-making duties were only limited by his creativity and tolerance for entrepreneurial rigor, which are inhumanly high, maybe even mutant-like. Hacking is both a science and art to David – it is deeply personal.

"You can't expect students to explore and find new things if [teachers and school administration] are only convergent thinkers," David argues.

In his view, convergence is a way of looking at problems that prioritize sameness, consolidation, and terminality. Convergence wants to get to the end of things—it is reductionist, it wants things done. David considers convergence a necessary but insufficient perspective.

> "We design multiple solutions that are relevant and context-based."

To explore problems deeply, David believes adults must also push for and model innovative "divergent" behaviors, ones that prioritize and create dynamic learning spaces driven by a "culture of experimentation." The continuous pressure on teachers and students for efficiency, standardization, and conformity are too industrial, he explains.

> "During divergence we are *creating* choices and during convergence we are *making* choices...I like the idea of creating choice. It not only allows for the probability of more creative solutions, but it also expands one's locus of control."

Overreliance on convergent processes subverts nonlinear creative processes and community building that are necessary to meet our societies' most wicked problems. David references Paulo Freire, William Grose, Octavia Butler, Nina Simone, and John Dewey as he shares his values. Each of them, he notes, manifested ideas and evolved collective thought in the context of their respective domains. He emphasizes that students and teachers need flexible space, mobility, and online supports to try new things. They must have the opportunity to create meaning for themselves based on their identity, values, networks, and prior learning. He is acutely aware of the interconnectedness of community, environment, relationships, technology, and place. Each comprises a key area he suggests is necessary to help students and teachers push beyond themselves and into new worlds of science, art, and sociality.

> "My only job was to innovate. Almost from day one, [my program] was new. Something that we got to create—it wasn't handed to us. We were given a canvas."

A crucial part of TAF's secret sauce is giving what Trish Millines Dziko calls a 'sandbox.' In standard organizational terms, a sandbox is a broader imperative that specifies the work that is to be done at the highest level, how it connects to organizational goals and mission, and what primary resources should be allocated toward that effort. Everything else in between is at the workers discretion. A former TAF Staff member noted:

> "You start blazing the trail and sometimes it turns out to be a path that actually leads somewhere, other times it's

sort of like dead ends. Your kind of like figure out another way around, but ultimately, again, it's a place where you know you're able to sort of like throw ideas out there and truly pursue them."

The sandbox approach can work well for the pure entrepreneur, but it has also been the bane of many past employees who wanted more structure, consistency, and direction for their work at TAF. While most times executive leadership was fairly *laissez-faire*, there can also be a tenor of heavy, sometimes overbearing, guidance that prescribes how work gets done at the tactical level.

David chuckles, *"It wasn't always a blank canvas… sometimes it was mixed media."*

The inconsistency between open sandbox and heavy-handed coaching can be challenging for employees who are trying to orient themselves to TAF's dynamic work environment that can be highly intimidating. A current TAF staff member:

> *"I learned how to do my job slowly because I failed to ask question of everybody all the time. So, I asked some questions, but I was so worried of not looking like I knew how to do my job that I didn't ask that many questions initially or I wasn't sure who to go to and then as soon as I started asking questions it was like a no-brainer."*

There is a sharp learning curve for new staff and teachers and everyone in the community needs to be able to learn from each other's success and failures. Facilitating how people perceived and internalized success and failure was a crucial part of David's role. It requires a high level of intentionality around listening to where people are might be struggling and developing solutions to building their capacity. "It is an art and a science," David says.

David extends his metaphor of using 'art' and 'design' as ways to discuss both TAF and his current work. He never seems to tire from expounding on layer-after-layer of rich experiences that have garnered him notable recognition, including the winner of the Crosscut 2017 Courage Award in Technology and a finalist competing against former Microsoft executive, Paul Allen, for the GeekWire, "Geek of the Year" in 2015. David explains:

> "I've seen similar roles in other schools but never seen a formula like that. It was radical. As a hacker on campus, my job was to disrupt. It took a lot of finesse to flow within the administration, to flow within industry, and flow within students, parents, and TAF."

David uses flow as a verbal descriptor for multimodal movements and differentiated approaches to facilitation among various stakeholders. In sitting with him, David conjures a Slick Rick-esque narrative ability with a calm and patient cadence. It should needs to be codified into a podcast called "The Art of Hacking." He makes an analogy between early 70's disc-jockeys who repurposed turntables and microphones to give birth to a music genre called hip-hop; and the way this generation of student-hackers must learn to repurpose the Internet, social media, and emerging technologies to create better socioeconomic realities. Realities that sound, look, and feel different from the status quo hierarchies of race, class, gender, and ability we experience today.

For this to happen, he contends, our communities must learn to code virtual and augmented realities—and not at the expense of being able to "code" substance and meaning into our physical world. He is an enthusiast of Arduino, making, material engineering, and design, in as much as he is a student of asset-based community development (ABCD) and self-determination theory.

THE RISKS OF HACKING

In many ways, TAF always had elements of a culture of hacking starting with Trish and her willingness to defy convention and the established power structures of education to create TAF. When she designed and developed an organization focused on after-school programs that morphed into one that affects public education more broadly, that was a hack. Many of the ideas that TAF manifested have changed the lives of their students, staffs, and partner institutions including districts and corporations. Internally, however, the hacking has come with a cost. David and many TAF teachers acknowledge the benefits of hacking but also spoke candidly about the risks. As one former TAF executive noted in terms of TAF's culture of hacking:

> *"Structures do not get put in place to sustain growth."*

For some TAF staff, they appreciate the leniency that extended when a person takes a step to do the right thing by way of students and colleagues. For the most part, they explained:

> *"You don't get dinged for doing the right thing even if it takes more time. There are expectations that you will do the right thing by the kids and by your peers and it's gets shown."*

There is also the risk that too many new programs, ideas, and initiatives can clash or overwhelm students and teachers. In some cases, opportunities that result are not evenly distributed and can even seem to reproduce hierarchies that are familiar to traditional schools. A TAF teacher commented on their experience sharing that:

> *"I think TAFA did a great job of bringing community partners in but not of getting kids out unless it was a special opportunity like internships. I was just bummed that some of my students who were the weakest academically didn't get an opportunity to have those internships when they might have benefitted the most."*

In 2016, TAF Academy merged with Saghalie Middle School forming the new TAF@Saghalie. At the time, TAF Academy as a small school was working well, but it had not scaled into the network of schools as the vision initially planned, or perhaps how donors and the broader community would have liked to see to warrant growth investment. At the same time, the small school campus was busting at the seams from overcrowding and waiting lists for incoming cohorts were steadily growing. TAF made a highly controversial decision to terminate their small school functionally, and a new effort was launched with the vision to build on lessons from TAF Academy at a larger scale. It was bittersweet for many staff members and teachers. A former TAF staff member noted:

> "Like this is not TAF Academy 2.0, this is something totally different, and I think the framing of that was helpful in letting some of this emotional and psychological baggage go because it is close to home for people."

The reference to "TAF Academy 2.0" refers to a moment in the development of TAF Academy where the school got an essential reboot of both leadership and staff in one year. We framed the reboot as TAF Academy 2.0 to signify deliberate shifts in both program and culture that were necessary to build a coherent approach to teaching and learning on campus. The former manager stating that the move to TAF@Saghalie was not merely a reboot is significant. It underscores the perceived level of change that many teachers and staff felt regarding the highly controversial decision. A former TAF executive noted:

> "TAF is no longer the small little shop that it once was where, again, I think it's, how do you reconcile the successes that we've had and the growth that we're enjoying with the realities of being able to be organized and structured accordingly?"

As TAF moves forward, there is a need to consider both the benefit and risk of hacking things as an innovation practice. A lesson from David was his commitment to breathe vibrancy and real-world relevance into the TAF Academy student body and adult teaching community. In theory, this meant David was to act as a liaison between TAF, TAF Academy, and influencers of Seattle's rich STEM community, including corporations and nonprofits such as Microsoft, Fred Hutchinson Cancer Research Center, Google, Amazon, and many others. In practice, this meant David did everything from co-teaching classes with teachers and transporting students up-and-down Interstate 5, to initiating an assortment of internships and service-learning opportunities to give students firsthand experiences in areas such as software development, video game design, entrepreneurship, making, and physical engineering. David's accomplishments during his five-year tenure at TAF were a pivotal cornerstone for how the school and organization have defined and approached STEM innovation ever since.

Conversations with Sherrell Dorsey

TAKING UP BLACK SPACE: SUPPORTING BLACK TECHNOLOGISTS AND ENTREPRENEURS BY LEVERAGING DATA JOURNALISM AND ECOSYSTEM DEVELOPMENT

Sherrell Dorsey is the Founder and CEO of both Black Tech Interactive and The Plug Daily newsletter, based in Charlotte, NC. In the early days of TAF, she was a student in the now-defunct Technical Teen Internship Program (TTIP) that was TAF's flagship program until 2005. As part of her TTIP experience (2001-2005), she completed four full-time summer internships at Microsoft, where each year she worked in Home and Auto MSN, on the SAAS team, as an assistant lab manager, and on the Diversity and Inclusion team, respectively. Sherrell describes her TAF experience as highly contributive to her career growth and trajectory as a data journalist, technologist, and social entrepreneur. Although her endeavors in academia and entrepreneurship have taken her across the country and globe, she stays connected to TAF and regularly checks-in on her frequent trips home to Seattle. For this book, I caught up with Sherrell a few times on her public-speaking trips to Seattle including an appearance on the "This is The Work" podcast pilot. I also visited her in Charlotte where I attended the grand opening of the Black Tech Interactive space, in the Camp North innovation and creativity hub. This chapter introduces content from our various conversations around our TAF experiences, journalism, technology ecosystem development, and her vision for how she intends to grow her startups.

SNAPSHOT OF SHERRELL DORSEY

Sherrell is always on the move. Monday, she might be on 125th in Harlem. On Wednesday, South Lake Union in Seattle. By Friday, she is back in her resident-hometown of Charlotte, NC., where she regularly convenes technologists, public officials, and other equity-minded members of the "Queen City" technology ecosystem. "I'm out here in these streets," Sherrell jokingly says regarding the rapid pace at which she routinely navigates diverse geographic and institutional terrains. It takes a lot of labor, long flights, networking and diligence to keep up with all the current and potential happenings in the global technology sector that have importance to Black communities. Sherrell is the type of person you can meet in-person today in Seattle, and then randomly discover through Instagram that she is in Frankfurt twenty-four hours later. All purpose, no pretense—Sherrell prides herself on keeping herself and others informed with content and experiences that are timely and relevant.

As Founder and CEO of both Black Tech Interactive and The Plug Daily newsletter, Sherrell leverages data to deliver interactive learning experiences and compelling news stories that inform and empower Black startup founders and technologists. Professionals across the country rely on Sherrell for timely updates on what is happening at the intersection of Black communities and technology; from the latest Black startup that was funded to announcements of grants and accelerator opportunities for entrepreneurs. Her updates and advice routinely encourage Black professionals to be present and actively engaged in rooms that often exclude Black people from tech information and opportunities. In one of her recent Tweets, Sherrell instructed her followers:

> "Keep sitting in rooms you don't believe you belong in until you feel comfortable taking up space."

The expression "Taking up space" recognizes key barriers to both access and belonging that Black innovators in the U.S. face when it comes to participating in high-growth technology markets. Despite a cacophony of corporate-driven rhetoric around diversity, inclusion, and equity, Black and many other nonwhite communities still contend with widespread lack of inclusion and leadership representation in the information and professional networks that drive and sustain mainstream technology innovation. These exclusive information and professional networks, both formal and informal, are overwhelmingly determinant to both how funds get allocated, and how decisions get made at prominent technology entities including companies, venture firms, industry associations, and government bodies. Rhere is a tragic and historically consistent reality occurring whereby exclusive information and professional networks that are seemingly impenetrable and often invisible to nonwhite innovators, in turn, all but dictate the context and opportunity landscape for nonwhite innovation, all without considering nonwhite voices and perspectives. With respects to her work, Sherrell encouraged her social media followers:

> "It baffles me when people ask, 'Is this only for black people?' Have you considered how often people in brown skin have been in rooms alone and no one blinked an eye? EVERY room where there is knowledge and information waiting is MY room. Belong in every room that will elevate you."

A primary value Sherrell brings to her work is creating pathways for Black professionals to be present and influential in the networks and rooms where technological information and opportunities often gets vetted and brokered. As a data journalist and ecosystem-developer, Sherrell develops spaces, narratives, and relationships that afford Black communities place, voice, and dynamic connection to the work of innovation. Much like Zora Neal Hurston (1935) did with her monumental book, <u>Mules to Men</u>, which was groundbreaking for showing what Black folklore looked like from "the inside-out," Sherrell's work often explicates the richness of Black technologists' work and stories to increase broader understanding of their value and connection to their work. Sherrell also uses her lived-experience as a torch to illuminate how just showing up as your authentic Black self in technology-focused meetups, conferences, classrooms, and boardrooms is both valuable and necessary, especially for Black women, who often get treated as outsiders. During one of our many phone conversations for this book, Sherrell reflected on her time in Bridgeport, CN working with Mayor Bill Finch. In that work, she enjoyed her impact but spoke to the challenges of isolation:

> "I was feeling isolated as a woman of color because there were very few of us in the room."

The isolation she describes echoes Trish and Dr. Joseph and many other Black women in tech and other high-growth industries. Her vision is to create an innovative model that demonstrates how diverse social actors (e.g., policymakers, business leaders, public media, community members) can work together to develop sustainable spaces that support Black, and similarly situated, innovators. She intends her model to be extensible to communities well beyond the United States, but her strategic focus on Black communities in the United States reflects her identity and intimate connection to specific sets of challenges Black communities face. Her work considers the current and potential roles of public data and policy, journalism, technology entrepreneurship, urban development, investment capital, education, and asset-based community development. To Sherrell, Black Tech Interactive is an urgent response to the dire need for physical-spaces that offer cultural affirmation and real-time informational relevance to Black startup founders and their collaborators. It is about creating space where people can be inspired to do their best work without having to overcome the culture of exclusion that permeates mainstream technology co-working and networking environments.

> "This is what I want to do for Charlotte, based on what I've seen people doing in other cities."

How does this complex work get done? Perhaps more than anything else, Sherrell is a world-class executor of what entrepreneurship literature refers to as bricolage—or the art of using whatever resources are available to achieve an outcome. Before moving to Charlotte, after graduating from Fashion Institute of Technology (FIT) in New York, Sherrell worked on green energy and education reform initiatives for Mayor Bill Finch in Bridgeport, Connecticut. Bridgeport faced significant resource challenges, but their leadership and community were determined to improve educational and environmental outcomes. The work meant sitting at tables where Sherrell did not always feel comfortable but overcoming those initial tensions to find her unique voice and value. That work also taught her invaluable lessons on how to innovate through resource scarcity.

In the United States, mainstream high-tech entrepreneurship happens in resource-rich, profit-driven contexts. Even if the entrepreneur in question is resource-strapped, the challenge in these contexts is typically one of access to available resources. Operating in resource-constrained settings is starkly different. Resource-constrained is a term that applies to contexts where the flow of funds to entrepreneurs is significantly impeded by physical or socially constructed barriers (e.g., geographic, institutional, sociopolitical, cultural). The challenge for entrepreneurs, in this case, is direr than access; it is availability. For many Black entrepreneurs and similarly situated social innovators, there is no doubt that longstanding patterns of anti-Blackness and institutional bias influence the availability of funding for Black entrepreneurs—and acutely so for Black women. Collecting and understanding the specific data narrative around this de facto boycott of Black technology entrepreneurship is central to Sherrell's mission.

SPACE MAKING AT BLACK TECH INTERACTIVE

I was honored to spend a couple of days with Sherrell for the grand opening of Black Tech Interactive's first community space, located in the city's planned Smart Innovation District in Charlotte's North End neighborhood off Statesville Avenue. It is worth noting that the new home for Black Tech Interactive is, as Issa Rae might say, everything Black! It is an open space, approximately 1200 square feet, with luminous glass garage doors, located in a picturesque historic complex that was once used to make armaments during WWII, and later as a distribution center for a national retailer. As we approached the entrance, an old brick façade gave the space a strength and permanence, while modern wood and metal accents created a textured sense of time-travel. We overheard one attendee refer to the collaborative area as a "photographer's playground."

Want to talk interior design? The décor of Black Tech Interactive's new space is an Afrofuturistic homage to Black aesthetics embedded with nuanced cultural symbolism. Modest but carefully curated furniture hints at both linguistic and semiotic textures that reference the African diaspora and instantiate both a living Black history and future. A wicker "peacock" chair nestled in a corner conjures the proud self-determination of Huey P. Newton; while along the wall, a futuristic mural of a black Femme image puts the voice of Nina Simone on your heart and the "Universal Consciousness" of Alice Coltrane on your brain. Impressions of a family and home extend from giant grandmotherly floor plants that whisper biology lessons from Flemmie Pansy Kittrell and George Washington Carver. And for anyone lost in the space, an intentionally curated stack of cultural-political literature is within arm's reach of every sitting station in the room—book titles such as Pedagogy of the Oppressed and The Black Jacobins—so that you can stay woke! All the while, rhythmic energy reverberates off the walls and makes you feel as if you are sitting in the shared workspace of Octavia Butler, Harriet Tubman, Madam C.J. Walker, Beyoncé, and Zora Neal Hurston. The appearance and existence of the space is not luck, however. Sherrell is a meticulous strategist, organizer, and planner.

> "I spent the last seven years researching and learning about how these systems work. Now I have all these templates

and models."

Black Tech Interactive a contemporary sociotechnical masterpiece. It is Black woman greatness in-progress; offering contagious, innovative, spiritual nourishment to everyone who enters. Vi Lyles, Charlotte's first Black woman mayor, was on site for the grand opening and spoke highly complimentary words about the visionary courage and necessity of the Black Tech Interactive space and movement.

THE PLUG DAILY – DATA JOURNALISM

Sherrell has remained curious on her entrepreneurial journey; one that took her from Seattle to New York, Bridgeport (Connecticut), and then Charlotte, to New York where she recently received a degree in Data Journalism from Columbia, and now back to Charlotte. As the Founder and CEO of The Plug—a daily newsletter covering black startups, founders, and innovators— Sherrell relishes the Columbia experience as a space to evolve her already gifted data-oriented storytelling.

> "I am responsible for using my voice to ensure there is a vast representation of a people that are not being documented in a way that is fair to their contributions to society."

Before launching The Plug, Sherrell's journalistic work had been published in Fast Company, The Atlantic's City Lab, The Root, and Next City. Her value for the untold stories of Black entrepreneurs and technologists stems childhood experience such as those at TAF (Seattle), and from her early realization that there was, and still is, an acute shortage of mainstream tech reporting about self-agency and autonomy in Black communities.

"The newsrooms are majority white."

While she discusses the under-representation of Black tech journalist as problematic, Sherrell has been encouraged by the consistent feedback she has gotten from editors and readers that her voice is appreciated. Thousands of people look to Sherrell each day as a nationally trusted voice for bringing nuance and depth to critical matters relevant to the growth and future of vibrant Black communities; from urban policy, sustainability, and education, to cryptocurrency, transportation, and artificial intelligence. Unlike many personalities on social media, however, Sherrell is not someone who mistakes volume for value.

When asked about her childhood and how she initially developed an interest in entrepreneurship and journalism, she half-embarrassingly laughs, "I was always observing the most random things."

Her home life also planted seeds. "Writing was a form of discipline in my house." At times when Sherrell got in trouble, her mom instilled in her habits of writing about her behaviors and reflecting on how she would change them. She has also benefited from having great entrepreneurial-minded mentors like Trish Millines Dziko along the way.

Sherrell considers both her writing and social entrepreneurship as harmonizing pillars of her life's work. Reflecting further on her childhood influences and time at TAF, she humbly states, "This is all I know how to do."

Much like Black Twitter and allies waiting on a real-world Wakanda, we are excited to imagine the impact Sherrell will have when some conscious investor or capital stakeholder realizes that a sizable direct investment toward her vision is precisely the type of win we all need. Not just for Charlotte, not only for Black communities but because it is necessary to shift our struggling democracy towards sociotechnical sustainability and innovation for us all. Ken Birdwell, the philanthropist, and longtime TAF supporter commented that the real value of TAF is its alumni and the potential they pose as the next generation of social innovators and problems solvers. According to Ken, it is not merely that the system is broken and unfair to nonwhite students and families, it is a more significant issue that the exclusion of nonwhite communities from innovation economies and markets mean broader society loses out on their genius. Ken is right too; visionary talents like Sherrell are precisely what is needed to move us all forward.

TAKING UP SPACE IN TECHNOLOGY ECOSYSTEMS

Sherrell explains "taking up space" as necessary work for changing the status quo marginalization of Black and nonwhite people in U.S. technology and innovation sectors. Data persistently show that Black people are grossly underrepresented in tech college majors, career pathways, and receive fewer opportunities and resources for entrepreneurship and innovation (Beasley, 2011; Dorsey, 2016; Green & Pryde, 1996; Harvey, 2005). For example, a report by the Information Technology and Innovation Foundation (ITIF) that tracked U.S. patent applications and recipients of several prominent innovation awards, found that nonwhite groups make up just 8 percent of "innovators" born in the U.S., of which Black contributed just .3 percentage points (Nager, Hart, Ezell, & Atkinson, 2016). Similarly, Mervis (2015) found that of $750 million-dollars in grant funds provided the Small Business Innovation Research (SBIR) program ran by National Institutes of Health (NIH), less than .5 percent went to Black primary investigators. It is important because the SBIR grants program is the nations' largest source of "undiluted" funds for research and innovation. SBIR is recognized by industry insider mainly as the last stage before commercialization. Undiluted means that funds are given to SBIR grant recipients without exchange for equity, unlike the case with venture capital. In the end, SBIR grant recipients get to retain a greater ownership stake in their companies and innovations. Datapoints such as the ITIF report support Sherrell's sentiment that Black people should persist in their entrepreneurship efforts, but the data also suggest inequities in the ways access to innovation resources are perceived and brokered at the institutional level. Furthermore, highly-publicized data on innovation often defines innovation in ways that create deficit narratives for Black, Latinx, and Native communities. These data overlook the types of innovation that Black communities contribute to a broader society that might serve our communities' stability, but are not valued and recognized by large funders, government agencies, and big philanthropy.

In *A Guide To Creating A Neighborhood Information Exchange: Building Communities by Connecting Local Skills and Knowledge*, Kretzmann and McKnight (1998) emphasize that it is necessary to take an asset-based community development (ABCD) approach in building capacity in impoverished communities. This type of approach begins with mindfulness about community ownership of solutions and seeks to amplify the voices and agency of community stakeholders rather than 'distal actors' in capacity development and change efforts. For example, production of this book can be considered an asset-based approach because this effort started with, and was led by, embedded members of the TAF extended community. Similarly, building an ecosystem is a dialogic practice, which means numerous stakeholders voices must be heard and respected for any meaningful change to take place. Trish and Jill took similar approaches in the early days of TAF. TAF cofounder Jill Dziko commented on her experiences:

> "Those were the days of a lot of going out into the community and talking to people about what they were doing and trying not to replicate, [talking about] what was happening in the community, how they were serving kids, and how we could be a part of that and add to that."

Jill's comments show how communities and their voices need to be at the forefront of community development efforts, whether an after-school program, school, or community information hub. In ecosystems development, the same value applies. The first step in working within a community is to not merely consult, but to request permission to be present and walk with those who are already empowered and working in those communities to affect change before any new intervention is applied – particularly interventions coming from the outside. A TAF Academy teacher spoke of their understanding of the role TAF played in facilitating their access to the community in their work, and how they see that as exemplary for types of relationships that should exist between districts, communities, and schools:

> "So often our teachers are coming from communities that are not the ones that they are working in, so I think leaders can build those partnerships with the community. Community organizations, community businesses, immersing teachers in the places that students live and function so that they have a much deeper understanding of not just the issues because we always go to issues, but all

the assets that are there for our kids."

Investment is center stage in the development of more equitable ecosystems. For investors and philanthropists who value equity and community-led innovation, this is the work. In Trish's case of launching TAF, relationships with philanthropists including Ken Birdwell and families such as the Ballmer and Gates families is a fortunate exception, not the norm for the vast majority of nonwhite founders. Even more extraordinary, however, and a testament to TAF's impact, is that several TAF alumni like Sherrell and other former TAF employees are now walking in Trish's footsteps as social innovators and ecosystem builders. Whereas Trish had personal capital and could rely on her wealthy Microsoft networks, Sherrell is working to build Black Tech Interactive and The Plug Daily from the ground up. Attracting investment presents unique challenges that she is determined to overcome. Sherrell is a primary example of TAF's potential to grow from a local social innovation tree that was planted in Seattle in 1996, into a burgeoning forest that stretches across the nation.

Part Four: Discussion on the Work Moving Forward

The final section of this book bridges ideas from previous sections toward a unifying perspective that considers identity, critical race and pedagogical theories, hacking, space-making, and knowledge-work in technology ecosystems for nonwhite peoples. The discussion frames broad ideas around *epistemic justice* as a call-to-action for STEM educators and those working around social innovation to increase their focus on, and support of, nonwhite and Indigenous knowledge and knowledge-systems including formal and informal variants. The book closes with parting questions and recommendations for future work and research.

Knowledge Production and Sharing is "The Work"

We asked contributors and community members to reflect on what does their TAF experience mean for them moving forward, and how do would they think about their legacy at TAF? Those close to TAF often ask, why are Trish and TAF not more nationally recognized names in the space of STEM education and social innovation? Why have not the lessons and experiences from the likes of David Harris, Sherrell Dorsey, Dr. Nicole Joseph, and many others been shared a more broadly? A big part of the answer lies in externalities such as difficult a funding climate and or shifts education policy. The bigger part of the answer, though, is because hardly anyone, including authors and contributors, has been afforded the proper time, resources, and opportunity to engage in rigorous knowledge production and sharing work. Underneath the surface of all our task lists, sticky notes, emails, and technology spurred productivity that churn TAF programs, there is a broader question relevant to the external and internalized oppression for nonwhite and Indigenous peoples which is, how can we value our internal knowledge, ways-of-knowing, and ways of being-and-doing, and knowers enough to pass on knowledge through regular and intergenerational changes in community membership and leadership? How can we understand the value of thoughtful knowledge-behaviors and knowledge-succession across a multitude of forms that range from institutional to informal practices?

DEVALUATION OF NONWHITE AND INDIGENOUS KNOWLEDGE

The devaluation and erasure of nonwhite and Indigenous communities' knowledge, ways-of-knowing, and knowledge-holders are primarily rooted in colonial histories that have instituted different systems of education and meaning-making (e.g., schools, media, popular press) in efforts to force various nonwhite populations to be better subjects of colonialism (Grande, 2015; Patel, 2016; Watkins, 2001). This is true whether we are talking about Native and Indigenous children who were taken from their parents and sent to Indian boarding schools where they learned to be "civilized" (Grande, 2015), or the influence of notable figures such as Samuel Chapman Armstrong, founder of the historically Black college, Hampton University, who William Watkins (2001) notes innovated education for Black people based on the idea that it was necessary to make them better, albeit racially inferior, subjects of industrial democracy. Both examples show the centrality of knowledge-systems in the ongoing colonization of nonwhite and Indigenous peoples. Beyond the topics most often discussed under "schools" and "education," this study of TAF internal members suggests nonwhite peoples and their supporters will benefit from revisiting critical conversations about underlying values, assumptions, beliefs, and practices around knowledge: What are they? How are they informed? By what and whom? And, how do they relate to our ideas about, and relationships to, power and self-determination, or lack thereof?

What are the core tensions (e.g., ideological, relational) that we need to recognize and resolve around how we value, conceptualize, access, and apply knowledge amongst ourselves and others? And at what scale(s) and through what types of structures are deep knowledge-work possible? For TAF and similar situated organizations, there are vital implications for sustainability.

REVISITING THIS BOOK AS AN EXHIBITION AND CASE-STUDY

Recall from the Introduction that this book is a public exhibition. It can also serve as a case-study in nonwhite knowledge-practices. Here, it is important to note that the self-publication of this book is partly the result of an *epistemic tension* at TAF – or, a stress resulting from differences in how knowledge is valued, produced, and shared by different peoples. In this book's case, there has been epistemic ambiguity and tension around how different TAF stakeholders understand and appreciate what it means for nonwhite communities and organizations such as TAF to produce programmatic outcomes, such as in a commercial sense, versus what it means for our communities to create knowledge. The epistemic tension was unexpected but the perhaps most remarkable discovery in this work.

To elaborate, knowledge production in many nonwhite and Indigenous communities often focuses on in-depth understanding of the people, relationships, and processes that produce knowledge. There is a high value placed on the internal knowledge-systems, practices, and ways-of-knowing that sustain nonwhite and Indigenous communities (Smith, 1999; Strega & Brown, 2015). Our primary modes of producing knowledge are often narrative-driven and highly contextualized within personal relationships. In these relationships, trust and access usually go hand-in-hand. In other words, no trust, no access. Recall that for the entirety of the United States history, colonial momentums have sought the commodification of nonwhite and Indigenous peoples' labor and knowledge (see Patel, 2016; Smith, 1999). In modern times, commodification often looks like the packaging of nonwhite labor and knowledge into consumable cultural products for the public sphere such as books, apps, programs, and initiatives.

On the one hand, these products are assets that can be easily brokered to support fundraising and advocacy efforts, but on another, they can reinforce toxic power-hierarchies and narratives because mainstream value-systems and institutions often drive their development and consumption (see Patel, 2016; Smith, 1999). As nonwhite communities have become more aware of these patterns of exploitation, internalized and external, an ethical burden exists around what knowledge is safe to collect, share, how, with whom, and under what circumstances? Those familiar with the concept of "intellectual property" might empathize with the dilemma. Nonwhite people are among the most researched peoples on the planet. Critical Theory and decolonizing methods prompts us ot ask, to what end does all the research serve and who benefits most? How can nonwhite and Indigenous peoples and organizatins best benefit from their knowledge-work? What are the barriers and opportunities? These are complex ethical questions that are not discussed nearly enough in mainstream education discourses.

One concluding reflection on this book is this: nonwhite and white leaders, philanthropic institutions, organizations, and investors must do more – to both understand and make substantial and sustained investments in nonwhite knowledge-production and knowledge-systems. These are the often invisible (i.e., tacit) activities and relationships that silently enable organizations like TAF to thrive. When asked about TAF's legacy, one staff member deftly stated:

> "I think the legacy of TAF is closely related to the people who work here, closely related to the people who pull these programs off, the relationships that have been established both within the staff, across the staff, with the staff and the students. It's pretty amazing to work in a place where so many of the people who were here at the beginning are still around here."

Inside and outside the organization, this is the deep knowledge work fuels the growth and development of nonwhite peoples, organizations, and communities, but often gets overlooked because we overemphasize deficit-based work and "fixing" what we perceive as broken – and this "fix it" mentality is both an internally and externally driven phenomena for many nonwhite peoples. We need knowledge "products" such as this book, and our programs and models, but it equally if not more important at this juncture in time to invest deeply in deep knowledge-work and the people, processes, and knowledge-systems that sustain our plights toward self-determination. But how does that work happen, where, and what does it look like?

A CALL FOR EPISTEMIC JUSTICE

Epistemic justice is a response to the reality that nonwhite communal and organizational knowledge and ways-of-knowing are not equitably valued, either in education or the broader United States society. We need a shift toward a more holistic knowledge-production perspective that more thoughtfully integrates nonwhite knowing-and-doing on our own terms. In this new paradigm, investment is spent to create space and time so that nonwhite peoples and communities can do the heavy lifting of healing and safely creating, exchanging, and sharing knowledge as they see best fit to support their own goals. In the parlance of software, we need to develop both frontend and backend solutions to how we produce and engage in knowledge-work; including those works that are open to the public and those that are proprietary. This is the groundbreaking work that Sherrell Dorsey does with Black Tech Interactive in Charlotte; this is how David D. Harris and I worked with our community to launch Hack the CD; and this is what Dr. Nicole M. Joseph experienced at Zion Preparatory

Academy and works to replicate in her work with teachers; this is what we all contributed to the growth and success of TAF and TAF Academy. In different ways and modes, we all are engaged in the invisible work of hacking knowledge-systems, or *knowledge-hacking*.

THE LABOR OF KNOWLEDGE

Epistemic justice and knowledge-hacking is more than tampering with what or how things are taught within the constructs of schools. Epistemic justice grapples with core matters of what is known, what is knowable, how, where, by whom, and at what costs? To keep it "100," knowledge is not free. There are multiple forms of labor that need to be considered when thinking about nonwhite knowledge and knowledge-systems, including the real and imagined value of efforts such as this book or any other knowledge-centered project. Beyond the direct physical labor to produce knowledge products and programs – due to the overarching context of patriarchal white supremacy – nonwhite people are engaged in a range of seemingly invisible and often uncompensated knowledge-labor just to survive. Many of us are doing the equivalent work of graduate studies on the side to make sense of our communities and context, and then running ourselves into the ground just to make a contribution. Increasingly, we need to examine areas of affective and digital labor as relevant sites where nonwhite peoples and their knowledge are exploited and undervalued.

DIGITAL LABOR AND KNOWLEDGE

There is an important ethical issue raised here. The issue is nonwhite peoples' agency to decide what knowledge and information gets shared, when, how, and to whom. This issue harkens back to early colonial times when nonwhite and Indigenous peoples were researched and explored by white settlers as a primary strategy for understanding how to disrupt and colonize their ways-of-being, knowledge systems, and communities. In this light, data-mining that disproportionately targets nonwhite people is not necessarily a new practice but perhaps merely the next wave of colonial momentum that needs redressing across digital domains. How do we mobilize our communities to understand what is potentially at stake with each swipe, click, and "like" on social media and the Internet? What does it mean that corporations and government have near "Cerebro-like[4]" access to our innermost conversations and personal networks. The conversation is an uphill battle, but one that starts with holistically educating students and families about the shape and structure of the digital worlds in which they participate and inhabit. Understanding the power of their knowledge and labor in these domains is key.

---

[4] Cerebro is computerized intelligence that gives Dr. Charles Xavier the power to telepathically see and connect with all humans and mutants in the world.

TAF IS A UNIQUE SITE FOR EXPLORING THE SOCIOTECHNICAL

TAF's work is unique. This book considers TAF's history and unapologetic approach to education rooted in the empowerment of nonwhite communities. Since 1996, TAF has cut across traditional sectors and evolved to become an informal community incubator where students and adults gain invaluable knowledge and practice in STEM innovation. Key stories have been shared and thoughtfully curated to illuminate key ideas, strategies, structures, and decisions that went into making TAF a highly-valued community asset in Washington State.

Trish is not a critical theorist or steeped in critical pedagogy, but her focus on making sure that TAF was built by nonwhite teachers and educators paved the way for those with more critical lenses such as Dr. Joseph and myself to bring critical epistemologies and practices into the TAF community of teachers and learners. Similarly, Trish defied convention in creating TAF as a space that was open to people from a myriad of backgrounds and networks, but she often put herself on the line to give us license to do "the work." Jill Dziko stated it best:

> "I mean this all hasn't been rainbows, sunshine, and unicorns and it's been tough for Trish because she's the face. She has taken a lot of flak because she's so out there. She's in the community, and people don't realize how much she's taken from the community, districts, and other

people."

Trish has modelled for technology companies and colleagues what can be done when we approach education and innovation from places that are rooted in a strong sense of identity, community, and place. Her actions set the stage for others to do the same and create space for others – including Sherrell Dorsey, David D. Harris, Nicole Joseph, me, and many others. TAF's knowledge-work included various forms of bricolage as described by David Harris, that resulted in a culture of people working outside of established orthodoxies and institutional prescriptions for how things should be done. Trish modelled her best self as a DIY person and entrusted others to be their best on behalf of our students.

Conclusion

In this project, as with any research, what makes it to print is only a small fraction of the work and knowledge that gets created and performed in the process of composition. With this book, both in content and its development process, I have done my best to strategically surface and create bridges around the epistemic value of TAF's work. Though it is presented to the public, this book serves as a grounding cornerstone of a necessary work that TAF and similarly situated organizations must take up toward intentional community-based, knowledge production and sharing.

Given our context, we can safely assume that hardly anything is in a preferred state. There is much work to be done and the pathways to moving things from one state to the next often go through programs and organizations – TAF is key example. In my work at TAF, however, I learned that people do not invest in programs, they invest in theory – theories of change and theories of action. Shifting the state of things is all about making a theoretical leap about how to get from the current state to a preferable state, and then convincing others to take that bold leap with you. Despite every evidence to the contrary, I am not convinced that this country has to be as it is today. We can do better – and by the way, we are sure that there is no golden era in the historical rearview that society needs to revisit. Student and adult education on both social and technical matters is, as Watkins (2005) points out, inherently poltical. We believe a logical starting place for "the work" is emancipatory sociotechnical education of those who have been most adversely affected by colonial practices. This work includes nonwhite communities educating themselves and their closest accomplices who may still operating under harmful habits of colonization, as most of us are – authors included – on lesson gleaned from Critical Theory, Black Feminist Thought, decolonizing methds, and critical perspectives on technology. TAF is well positioned to pursue this work.

As both a first-time and the lead author on this book, I can assure that this book keeps in line with TAF's history of unconventionality – starting with the process for producing and publishing this work, to this unpredictable conclusion. It was a tremendous challenge, but ultimately it has been rewarding and pushed me further into my own reflection and reflexivity for both this and my future work and research. I am thankful to Trish and others for both the opportunity to have worked on this book with my community, and for pushing me through the countless hours of hard work it took to produce it. It represents a functional capstone for my work as a practitioner at TAF, and in doing so, also instantiates my transition into a publicly-engaged scholar focused on the roles of knowledge, information systems, education, and innovation amongst our peoples.

On behalf of TAF, Trish, our contributors, and extended community – be at peace.

Appendix I: References

Abbate, J. (2012). *Recoding gender: women's changing participation in computing.* Cambridge, Massachusetts: MIT Press.

Alexander, M. (2010). *The new Jim Crow: Mass incarceration in the age of colorblindness.* New York: The New Press.

Al-Hardan, A. (2014). Decolonizing Research on Palestinians: Towards Critical Epistemologies and Research Practices. *Qualitative Inquiry, 20*(1), 61–71. https://doi.org/10.1177/1077800413508534

Almirall, E., Lee, M., & Majchrzak, A. (2014). Open innovation requires integrated competition-community ecosystems: Lessons learned from civic open innovation. *Business Horizons, 57*(3), 391–400. https://doi.org/10.1016/j.bushor.2013.12.009

Anderson, J. D. (2014). *The Education of Blacks in the South, 1860-1935.* Chapel Hill, UNITED STATES: University of North Carolina Press. Retrieved from http://ebookcentral.proquest.com/lib/washington/detail.action?docID=880026

Anna Stahlbrost, B. B.-K. (2011). Exploring users motivation in innovation communities. *Int. J. of Entrepreneurship and*

Innovation Management, 14(4). https://doi.org/10.1504/IJEIM.2011.043051

Banks, J. A., & Banks, C. A. M. (2004). *Handbook of research on multicultural education* (2nd ed.). San Francisco, CA: Jossey-Bass.

Beasley, M. A. (2011). *Opting out: losing the potential of America's young black elite.* Chicago: The University of Chicago Press.

Berry, D. M. D. M. (2014). *Critical theory and the digital.* New York: Bloomsbury.

Bonilla-Silva, E. (2001). *White supremacy and racism in the post-civil rights era.* Lynne Rienner Publishers.

Bonilla-Silva, E. (2017). *Racism without racists: Color-blind racism and the persistence of racial inequality in America.* Rowman & Littlefield.

Collins, P. H. (1989). The Social Construction of Black Feminist Thought. *Signs, 14*(4), 745–73. https://doi.org/10.1086/494543

Collins, P. H., & Bilge, S. (2016). *Intersectionality.* Cambridge, UK ; Malden, MA: Polity Press. Retrieved from https://www.wiley.com/en-us/Intersectionality-p-9780745684499

Connelly, F. M., & Clandinin, D. J. (1990). Stories of Experience and Narrative Inquiry. *Educational Researcher*, *19*(5), 2–14. https://doi.org/10.3102/0013189X019005002

Crenshaw, K. (1989). Demarginalizing the intersection of race and sex: a Black feminist critique of antidiscrimination doctrine, feminist theory, and antiracist politics. *The University of Chicago Legal Forum*, *140*, 139–167.

Crenshaw, K. W. (2011). Twenty years of critical race theory: looking back to move forward. (Critical Race Theory: A Commemoration). *Connecticut Law Review*, *43*(5), 1253–1352.

Davis, C.-S. (1996). *The equity equation: fostering the advancement of women in the sciences, mathematics, and engineering* (1st ed.). San Francisco: Jossey-Bass Publishers.

Dorsey, S. (2016, January 21). Black Women VCs Are Challenging The Culture Of The Investment Industry. Retrieved July 17, 2016, from http://www.fastcoexist.com/3055667/black-women-vcs-are-challenging-the-culture-of-the-investment-industry

Duarte, M. E. (2017). *Network Sovereignty: Building the Internet across Indian Country*. University of Washington Press.

Dunaway, W. A. (2003). *The African-American family in slavery and emancipation.* New York: Maison des Sciences de l'homme/Cambridge University Press.

Emdin, C. (2016). *For White Folks Who Teach in the Hood... and the Rest of Y'all Too: Reality Pedagogy and Urban Education.* Beacon Press.

Eubanks, V. (2011). *Digital dead end: fighting for social justice in the information age.* Cambridge, Massachusetts: MIT Press.

Eubanks, V. (2018). *Automating inequality: how high-tech tools profile, police, and punish the poor* (First edition.). New York, NY: StMartin's Press.

Fanon, F. (1963). *The Wretched of the Earth* (40th Printing edition). New York: Grove Press.

Feenberg, A. (1991). *Critical theory of technology.* New York: Oxford University Press.

Feenberg, A. (2002). *Transforming Technology A Critical Theory Revisited* (2nd ed.). Oxford: Oxford University Press, USA.

Finnery, K., & Rencher, M. (2016). *The real unicorns of tech: Black women founders.* Digital Undivided.

Freire, P. (1993). *Pedagogy of the oppressed* (New rev. 20th-Anniversary ed.). New York: Continuum.

Garibay, J. C. (2013). Achieving equity within and beyond STEM. In R. T. Palmer & D. C. Maramba (Eds.), *Fostering Success of Ethnic and Racial Minorities in STEM: The Role of Minority Serving Institutions* (p. 209). Retrieved from https://books.google.com/books?hl=en&lr=&id=eo6gPEFGbYUC&oi=fnd&pg=PA209&dq=Achieving+Equity+Within+and+Beyond+STEM&ots=1znDQzj7IO&sig=FBgLcsYK6vEQwz5xVKI8vwklrH0

Grande, S. (2015). *Red pedagogy: Native American social and political thought* (Tenth anniversary edition.). Lanham: Rowman & Littlefield. Retrieved from http://search.ebscohost.com/login.aspx?direct=true&scope=site&db=nlebk&db=nlabk&AN=1057151

Green, S., & Pryde, P. (1996). *Black Entrepreneurship in America.* Transaction Publishers, Rutgers University New Brunswick, NJ 08903 paperback: ISBN-1-56000-885-7, $2195; clothbound: ISBN-0-88738-290-8.

Grönlund, H. (2011). Identity and Volunteering Intertwined: Reflections on the Values of Young Adults. *VOLUNTAS: International Journal of Voluntary and Nonprofit*

Organizations, 22(4), 852–874.
https://doi.org/10.1007/s11266-011-9184-6

Grossman, J. M., & Porche, M. V. (2014). Perceived Gender and Racial/Ethnic Barriers to STEM Success. *Urban Education, 49*(6), 698–727. https://doi.org/10.1177/0042085913481364

Harvey, A. M. (2005). Becoming Entrepreneurs: Intersections of Race, Class, and Gender at the Black Beauty Salon. *Gender and Society, 19*(6), 789–808.

Hill, C., Corbett, C., & Rose, A. (2010). *Why so few? Women in science, technology, engineering, and mathematics.* American Association of University Women. Retrieved from https://eric.ed.gov/?id=ED509653

Hill Collins, P. (2010). The New Politics of Community. *American Sociological Review, 75*(1), 7–30. https://doi.org/10.1177/0003122410363293

hooks, bell. (1981). *Ain't I a woman: Black women and feminism.* Boston, MA: South End Press.

hooks, bell. (2000). *Feminism is for everybody: Passionate politics.* New York: Routledge.

Hurston, Z. N. (1935). *Mules and Men.* Philadelphia: J.B. Lippincott Company.

Jackson, S. N. (2012). *Creole Indigeneity*. Retrieved from https://www.upress.umn.edu/book-division/books/creole-indigeneity

Jackson, S. N. (2014, June 4). Humanity beyond the Regime of Labor: Antiblackness, Indigeneity, and the Legacies of Colonialism in the Caribbean [Decolonization: Indigeniety, Education, and Society]. Retrieved July 4, 2018, from https://decolonization.wordpress.com/2014/06/06/humanity-beyond-the-regime-of-labor-antiblackness-indigeneity-and-the-legacies-of-colonialism-in-the-caribbean/

John W. Creswell. (2007). *Qualitative inquiry & research design: choosing among five approaches* (2nd ed.). Thousand Oaks: Sage Publications.

Jordan, T. (2015). *Information politics: liberation and exploitation in the digital society*. London: Pluto Press.

Joseph, N. M. (n.d.). *Mathematizing Feminism: Black Girls' and Women's Experiences in the P-20 Mathematics Pipelines*. Boston, MA: Harvard Education Press.

Joseph, N. M., Hailu, M., & Boston, D. (2017). Black Women's and Girls' Persistence in the P–20 Mathematics Pipeline: Two Decades of Children, Youth, and Adult Education

Research. *Review of Research in Education, 41*(1), 203–227. https://doi.org/10.3102/0091732X16689045

Joseph, N. M., Haynes, C., & Cobb, F. (2016). *Interrogating whiteness and relinquishing power: white faculty's commitment to racial consciousness in STEM classrooms.* New York: Peter Lang.

Joseph, N. M., Jett, C. C., & Leonard, J. (2018). A Review of Cases for Mathematics Teacher Educators: Facilitating Conversations About Inequities in Mathematics Classrooms. *Journal for Research in Mathematics Education, 49*(2), 232. https://doi.org/10.5951/jresematheduc.49.2.0232

Karabey, C. N. (2012). Understanding Entrepreneurial Cognition through Thinking Style, Entrepreneurial Alertness and Risk Preference: Do Entrepreneurs differ from others? *Procedia - Social and Behavioral Sciences, 58*, 861–870. https://doi.org/10.1016/j.sbspro.2012.09.1064

Kendi, I. X. (2016). *Stamped from the beginning: The definitive history of racist ideas in America.* New York: Nation Books.

Kourti, I. (2016). Using personal narratives to explore multiple identities in organisational contexts. *Qualitative Research* in *Organizations and Management, 11*(3), 169–188. https://doi.org/10.1108/QROM-02-2015-1274

Krauthamer, B. (2013). *Black slaves, Indian masters: slavery, emancipation, and citizenship in the Native American south.* Chapel Hill: University of North Carolina Press.

Kretzmann, J. P., & McKnight, J. (1998). *A guide to creating a neighborhood information exchange: building communities by connecting local skills and knowledge.* Evanston, Illinois: The Asset-Based Community Development Institute, Institute for Policy Research, Northwestern University; Chicago, IL.

Krige, K., & Silber, G. (2016). *The Disruptors: Social entrepreneurs reinventing business and society.* Cape Town: ABC Press.

Leung, V., Alejandre, R. H., & Jongco, A. (2016). *Unequal access: How some California charter schools illegally restrict enrollment.* American Civil Liberties Union.

Lipsitz, G. (1998). *Possessive Investment In Whiteness* (1st edition). Philadelphia: Temple University Press.

Loomba, A. (2015). *Colonialism/Postcolonialism.* Hoboken: Taylor and Francis.

Marable, M. (1983). *How capitalism underdeveloped Black America: problems in race, political economy and society.*

Maragh, R. S. (2016). "Our Struggles Are Unequal": Black Women's Affective Labor Between Television and Twitter. *Journal of Communication Inquiry, 40*(4), 351–369. https://doi.org/10.1177/0196859916664082

Memmi, A. (1965). *The colonizer and the colonized.* Boston, MA: Beacon Press. Retrieved from https://books.google.com/books?hl=en&lr=&id=ee1TEf25qicC&oi=fnd&pg=PP1&dq=colonized+and+colonizer+memmi&ots=2e7mboBPOQ&sig=rfn2NjDJNPow0PhO1wU4oAb6q_8

Mervis, J. (2015). NIH program fails to launch blacks in biotech. *Science, 350*(6263), 896–896. https://doi.org/10.1126/science.350.6263.896

Mills, C. M. (1997). *The racial contract.* Ithaca: Cornell University Press.

Morrill, R. (2013). The Seattle Central District (cd) Over Eighty Years. *Geographical Review; New York, 103*(3), 315–335.

Nager, A., Hart, D., Ezell, S., & Atkinson, R. D. (2016). *The Demographics of Innovation in the United States.* Information Technology and Innovation Foundation.

Retrieved from http://www.inthekzone.com/report-ranking-images-pdfs/2016-demographics-of-innovation.pdf

Nakamura, L. (2002). *Cybertypes: race, ethnicity, and identity on the Internet.* New York: Routledge.

Nakamura, L., & Chow-White, P. (2012). *Race after the Internet.* New York: Routledge.

Noble, S. U. (2018). *Algorithms of oppression: how search engines reinforce racism.* New York: New York University Press.

Nonaka, I. (1995). *The knowledge-creating company: how Japanese companies create the dynamics of innovation.* New York: Oxford University Press.

Ollerenshaw, J. A., & Creswell, J. W. (2002). Narrative Research: A Comparison of Two Restorying Data Analysis Approaches. *Qualitative Inquiry, 8*(3), 329–347. https://doi.org/10.1177/10778004008003008

Oster, S. M. (1995). *Strategic management for nonprofit organizations: theory and cases.* New York: Oxford University Press.

Painter, N. I. (2010). *The History of White People.* New York, NY: Norton.

Palmer, R. T., Maramba, D. C., & Gasman, M. (Eds.). (2013). *Fostering success of ethnic and racial minorities in STEM: the role of minority serving institutions.* New York: Routledge, Taylor & Francis Group.

Patel, L. (2016). *Decolonizing educational research: from ownership to answerability.* New York: Routledge. Retrieved from http://site.ebrary.com/id/11136947

Pateman, C. (1988). *The sexual contract.* Stanford, Calif.: Stanford, Calif. : Stanford University Press.

Sakai, J. (2014). *Settlers: the mythology of the white proletariat from mayflower to modern.* Oakland, California: PM Press.

Sandoval, M., & Fuchs, C. (2010). Towards a critical theory of alternative media. *Telematics and Informatics, 27*(2), 141–150. https://doi.org/10.1016/j.tele.2009.06.011

Scholz, T. (2013). *Digital labor: the Internet as playground and factory.* New York, NY: Routledge. Retrieved from http://public.eblib.com/choice/publicfullrecord.aspx?p=10 47015

Shedd, C. (2015). *Unequal City: Race, Schools, and Perceptions of Injustice.* Russell Sage Foundation. Retrieved from https://muse.jhu.edu/book/41532

Smith, L. T. (1999). *Decolonizing methodologies: research and indigenous peoples*. London : Dunedin, N.Z.: Zed Books ; University of Otago Press.

Snelgrove, C., Dhamoon, R. K., & Corntassel, J. (2014). Unsettling settler colonialism: The discourse and politics of settlers, and solidarity with Indigenous nations. *Decolonization: Indigeneity, Education & Society, 3*(2), 1–32.

Sovacool, B. K., & Hess, D. J. (2017). Ordering theories: Typologies and conceptual frameworks for sociotechnical change. *Social Studies of Science, 47*(5), 703–750. https://doi.org/10.1177/0306312717709363

Stefancic, J. (1997). Latino and Latina critical theory: An annotated bibliography. *California Law Review, 85*(5), 1509–1584.

Stokes, D. E. (2011). *Pasteur's quadrant: Basic science and technological innovation*. Brookings Institution Press.

Strega, S., & Brown, L. (2015). *Research as resistance: revisiting critical, indigenous, and anti-oppressive approaches* (Second edition.). Toronto: Canadian Scholars' Press : Women's Press.

Tuck, E., & Yang, K. W. (2012). Decolonization is not a metaphor, 40.

Tuck, E., & Yang, K. W. (2013). *Youth resistance research and theories of change*. New York: Routledge. Retrieved from http://search.ebscohost.com/login.aspx?direct=true&scope=site&db=nlebk&db=nlabk&AN=669072

US Census Bureau. (2018). U.S. Census Bureau quickfacts: Seattle, Washington; UNITED STATES. Retrieved June 25, 2018, from https://www.census.gov/quickfacts/fact/table/seattlecitywashington,US/PST045217

U.S. Department of Labor. (2015). Table 1. Volunteers by selected characteristics, September 2015 [Government]. Retrieved July 16, 2018, from https://www.bls.gov/news.release/volun.t01.htm

Vaidhyanathan, S. (2011). *The Googlization of everything (and why we should worry)*. Berkeley: University of California Press.

Von Krogh, G. (2000). *Enabling knowledge creation: how to unlock the mystery of tacit knowledge and release the power of innovation*. Oxford ; New York: Oxford University Press.

Warner-King, K., & Price, M. (2004). *Legal issues and small high schools: strategies to support innovation in Washington State*. Center on Reinventing Public Education. Retrieved from http://eric.ed.gov/?id=ED485893

Watkins, W. H. (2001). *The White architects of Black education: ideology and power in America, 1865-1954*. New York: Teachers College Press.

Watkins, W. H. (2005). *Black protest thought and education*. New York: PLang.

Weber, K. (2011a). Role Models and Informal STEM-Related Activities Positively Impact Female Interest in STEM. *Technology & Engineering Teacher, 71*(3), 18–21.

Weber, K. (2011b). Role Models and Informal STEM-Related Activities Positively Impact Female Interest in STEM. *Technology & Engineering Teacher, 71*(3), 18–21.

Williams, H. A. (2007). *Self-Taught: African American Education in Slavery and Freedom*. The University of North Carolina Press.

Wolfe, P. (2006). Settler colonialism and the elimination of the native. *Journal of Genocide Research, 8*(4), 387–409. https://doi.org/10.1080/14623520601056240

Woodson, C. G. (2000). *The mis-education of the Negro* (1st ed.). Chicago, Ill.: African-American Images.

Appendix II: Reflection on "This is Work" by Zithri Ahmed Saleem

During the sixteen years I served by Trish's side, I got a privileged view of her approach(es) to leadership, politics, work relationships, management, and organizational development, including her uncompromising will to do whatever she felt must be done to sustain the organization. Trish, like TAF, is full of fighting spirit. The expression "force of nature" came up several times in interviews with people familiar with TAF's work. During my TAF tenure, I observed Trish in meetings, boardrooms, classrooms, and in numerous high-intensity settings where my role was often taking copious notes, providing strategic advice, or chiming in with educational expertise to our executive team, staff, and partners. The more I reflectively studied both Trish and the organization, the more I felt something needed to be written to capture the dynamic nature and value of TAF's work.

It was during a dinner conversation with longtime TAF supporters and my mentors, Sonja Gustafson, and her husband and business partner, Steve Trautman, that my vision for this work, and my eventual pursuit of a doctorate in information science, began to form. Sonja and Steve are former colleagues of Trish from her Microsoft days, and Sonja was the Social Venture Partners (SVP) liaison to TAF for the small grant that provided my salary when I was hired in 2000. Since my early days at TAF, Sonja and Steve have continuously, but gently, guided me toward a knowledge-management perspective both in my work at TAF and leading up my pursuit of a doctorate. It was them who first put me on a track that lead to scholarly thought-leaders in knowledge and organizational studies such as Nonaka, Ichijo, Von Krough, Drucker, Wenger, and Lave. Accordingly, much of my work at TAF was heavily influenced by a knowledge-perspective – or an approach that places primary importance on how and what people learn through their experiences at work, including how knowledge is created, applied, transferred, archived, accessed, and in worst cases, lost. Loss of organizational knowledge is a key contributor to lack of sustainability, effectiveness, and innovation (Nonaka, 1995; Oster, 1995; Von Krogh, 2000). A primary driver for me wanting to see TAF earnestly take up the work to write a book was my awareness and studies of organizational learning and knowledge management. I understood what seemed to be invisible to Trish and many others in the organization; that TAF was losing big chunks of what made it special. With each departure of high-impact staff, TAF was losing invaluable organizational knowledge and there were no systems or strategies in place to recoup or reinvest that knowledge back into the organization. Something needed to be done to bring awareness to the knowledge-management issue and suggest a strategy for managing it within the TAF organizational context.

Like many non-profits and educational organizations,

TAF has experienced periods of relatively high employee and teacher turnover, however, there have been several exceptions to that norm. A handful of people have had 5-year tenures or more, and some of these "TAF folk" contributed indispensable DNA to what has made TAF an award-winning innovator in STEM education. These folks, like I, possess insider knowledge few people have on what has driven both successes and many hard lessons-learned over TAF's twenty-plus years of operation. By way of its former staff and teachers - TAF has benefited from deep expertise in systems design, law, learning science, curriculum and instruction, educational policy, critical race theory, software development, and organizational management. This expertise has been indispensable to TAF's ability to navigate adverse institutional terrains that often stop well-meaning people from positively affecting public education and communities. During the build-up to launch TAF Academy, our education team would laughingly use the term "brute intelligence" in describing TAF's organizational approach —smart people who given time and resources can solve nearly any problem. It was not always pretty or efficient, but more times than not, things seemed to work out in ways that benefited our students, communities, and staff. Yet, even this approach has a limit. Firstly, it is nearly impossible to effectively scale because it requires significant time for people to "figure things out" and resources are scarce. Secondly, it can put strain on relationships, both internal and external, because specific outcomes can be harder to articulate at the outset of a project. This book is a class example! There was no way to accurately predict how this book or the overall effort would turnout because this level of knowledge production and community reflection was something entirely foreign to the organization.

I consider it a blessing to maintain deep, almost-familial relationships with many of my TAF folk even though we all have moved on from formal positions within the organization. Today, most of us stay connected and committed to the TAF mission, directly or indirectly, answering the bell each time the organization needs our support, or in this case, chiming in to ensure that the current generation of TAF staff, board members, teachers, students, and supporters have access to the best of our institutional knowledge and reflections through this book. With this book, we extend some of our key ideas and lessons to the current TAF internal and broader community of activists, teachers, policymakers, industry professional, and students who are engaged, or interested, in the work of STEM education social innovation.

In conceptualizing this book, the obvious themes around which to frame TAF's work might have been STEM education, curriculum, public schools, nonprofit management, or education policy. I considered all these focal points and many of them are indeed touched on in the chapters. However, in my review of related research over my first two-years of doctoral studies, and in consideration of ongoing reflections on my sixteen (16) years of TAF experience, the frame of social innovation seemed more appropriate given the frequency at which TAF defied conventional logic to serve thousands of students in its community. Along the way, TAF broke rules, defied logic, spurned convention, and created opportunities for both students and adults. As one former TAF development officer stated to me in an informal interview, "TAF really shouldn't be here." In talking about TAF, Dr. Robinson mentioned that it is one of few nonwhite-led organizations in the nation that has sustained expertise and demonstrated social innovation for over twenty (20) years.

As an organization, however, there were three key intentions behind TAF sponsoring the publication of this book. Firstly, TAF's norms and values call for all TAF community members to be engaged in making TAF a reflective, learning organization. Constant pressures of fundraising and programmatic operation, however, means there have been long stretches of times when TAF leadership has struggled to model continuous learning and improvement, including regular reflection upon, and interrogation of, its strategies, activities, and outcomes. Still, TAF leadership understands that every so often it is healthy for organizations to do a deep reflection that requires more time and resources than most small organizations can muster given demands of programs and fund development. At just north of 20-years-old as an organization, this book is a critical part of the work to sustain and evolve TAF's mission through a reflective organizational process. This book provokes critical conversations that surfaced during my two years (from 2016-18) of intentional research, writing, and preparation of these pages with TAF organizational stakeholders; and builds on my insights and experiences as a central organizational leader from 2000-2016.

The second organizational intention behind this book supports a key part of TAF's culture; an agreement between adults to model the learning behaviors expected of our students. This means we extend the project-based learning (PBL) framework we use to support our students to ourselves, which any TAF student can tell you requires a public exhibition. Student exhibition is an essential part of project-based learning because it invites feedback from the learning community and is an act of accountability. Exhibition strives to make internal work public, and in doing so share progress by making many key organizational intentions, actions, outcomes, and challenges available for consideration by, and feedback from, others – internal and external stakeholders alike. Thus, in writing this book as a self-published exhibition, TAF opens itself to the community and public feedback to deepen organizational learning. As lead author, I also extend my own experiences and perspectives for critique and analysis as well.

The third consideration for undertaking this book is to push TAF toward an intentional practice of knowledge-sharing with current and potential allies and accomplices. The two (2) years of focused-work to create this book is a pathway to the development of future books, podcasts, documentaries, and content that might inform and inspire audiences of all backgrounds. A major intention of this book is to build upon the honored tradition of nonwhite critical scholar-practictioners and educators who have engaged in the work of social innovation. Part of this work is putting ideas and solutions forth for public consumption and broader social benefit, even when those works might be unfinished, unpopular, or against the grain mainstream society. In working with the contributors to this effort, I have sought to merge our voices and perpectives along with additional members of our commuity who have been integral to TAF's sustained success. Our intention is to add this book to extant literature that calls for much needed disruption of status quo institutional practices and mindsets, including predominant ways of being, knowing, and doing around technology and innovation that are rooted in systems of patriarchy, white supremacy, ableism, and other forms of oppression.

Made in the USA
San Bernardino, CA
09 December 2018